SECRET
BANGKOK

Narina Exelby and Mark Eveleigh

JONGLEZ PUBLISHING

Travel guides

Narina Exelby is a freelance writer and editor who, in early 2012, swapped stability in Cape Town and 15 years in the international magazine industry for freedom and life on the road. She travels frequently – mostly around South-East Asia, Southern Africa and Europe – and while she has always been drawn to quiet spaces, she is often surprised by the delight she finds in the rhythm of big-city life. Bangkok tops Narina's list of favourite cities on the planet; she claims she could spend a lifetime of early mornings walking along the streets and canals, where she seeks out beauty in unexpected places.

Mark Eveleigh first hitch-hiked through Thailand almost 30 years ago, when elephants were still being ridden through the streets of Bangkok. He has since travelled throughout Thailand on magazine assignments more times than he can count and, with his partner Narina, has regularly been based in Bangkok over the years. *Secret Bangkok* was a welcome challenge – an opportunity to explore hidden locations that were, in many cases, unknown even to some of the most knowledgeable local guides.

While *Secret Bangkok* was designed to be an exciting, unexpected and eminently readable guide for any visitor to what might be the world's most exciting city, we have aimed to create a book that will also be revelation even for the most widely travelled "old hands".

Evocative descriptions of the locations are frequently coupled with thematic sections highlighting historical details or cultural anecdotes as an aid to understanding the city in all its complexity. Going far beyond the limitations of most guidebooks, *Secret Bangkok* reveals fascinating aspects of the city that are almost invariably overlooked by the outsider.

Comments on this guidebook and its contents, as well as information on places we may not have mentioned, are more than welcome and will enrich future editions.

Don't hesitate to contact us:
E-mail: info@jonglezpublishing.com
Jonglez Publishing, 25 rue du Maréchal Foch
78000 Versailles, France

BANGKOK: A TIMELINE OF KINGS

Some pages in this book contain references to different parts of Thailand's history, as well as to various kings. In order for that to make sense, this simplified history lesson might be useful.

Thailand or Siam?

Historically the tradition in Thailand was always to name the kingdom after its capital city, but in 1856 the country officially became Siam, a name used for the region since the 16th century. In 1939 the country's name changed to Thailand – "Land of the Free". In this book, when referring to events that took place before 1939, we use the name Siam.

Ayutthaya Period (1350 to 1767)

The Ayutthaya Kingdom covered much of what is Thailand today. War with neighbouring kingdoms was rife, but there was also a very rich culture and an appreciation for the arts during this time. Its capital, the city of Ayutthaya (70 km upriver from Bangkok, and well worth a visit), was almost completely destroyed by the Burmese in 1767.

Thonburi Period (1767 to 1782)

Taksin the Great (see p. 16) drove the Burmese out of Ayutthaya and established a new capital at Thonburi. It remained an independent province until 1971, when it merged into Bangkok.

Rattanakosin Period (1782 to present)

When General Chakri (posthumously named Rama I) took to the throne he moved the capital over the river to Rattanakosin Island, a piece of land between the Chao Phraya River and the Rop Krung Canal (see p. 21 and p. 22). Rattanakosin translates roughly as "Jewelled City", referring to the Emerald Buddha (see p. 64). The descendants of

Rama I, the Chakri Dynasty, have remained in power ever since – although an almost bloodless revolt in 1932 marked the end of an absolute monarchy and the beginning of a constitutional monarchy.

The Chakri Dynasty
There is a very complex system of titles and names in Thailand. People's names and (often very lengthy) titles changed and accumulated throughout their lives, depending on the positions they were born into or earned – or, in the case of women, the positions of the men they married. For ease of reference, in this book we have used the simplest and most widely used names, and refer to the kings by the title that is awarded posthumously, Rama, followed by the number of their succession. It was Rama VI who initiated this, and it has been common practice ever since.

- **Rama I:** Phraphutthayotfa Chulalok
  Reign: 1782 to 1809
- **Rama II:** Phraphutthaloetla Naphalai
  Reign: 1809 to 1824
- **Rama III:** Phranangklao
  Reign: 1824 to 1851
- **Rama IV:** Phrachomklao (also called Mongkut)
  Reign: 1851 to 1868
- **Rama V:** Chulalongkorn
  Reign: 1868 to 1910
- **Rama VI:** Vajiravudh (also called Phramongkutklao)
  Reign: 1910 to 1925
- **Rama VII:** Prajadhipok (also called Phrapokklao)
  Reign: 1925 to 1935
- **Rama VIII:** Ananda Mahidol (see p. 45)
  Reign: 1935 to 1946
- **Rama IX:** Bhumibol Adulyadej
  Reign: 1946 to 2016
- **Current monarch:** King Maha Vajiralongkorn
  Reign: 2016 to present

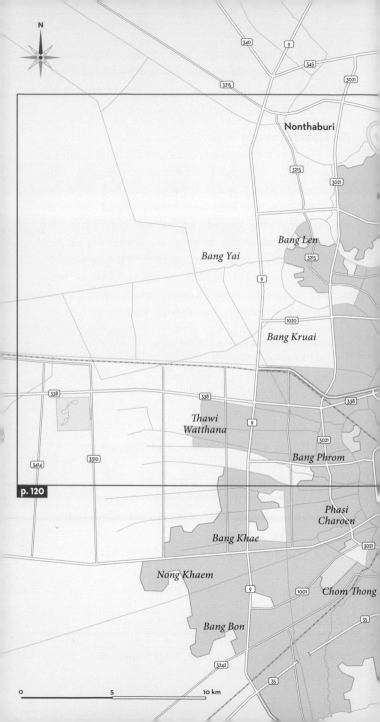

N

340
9
345
3021
3215

Nonthaburi

3215
3021

Bang Len

3215

Bang Yai

9

1020

Bang Kruai

338
338
338

Thawi Watthana

9

3021

Bang Phrom

3414
3310

p. 120

Phasi Charoen

3021

Bang Khae

Nong Khaem

9
1001
Chom Thong

35

Bang Bon

3242
35

0   5   10 km

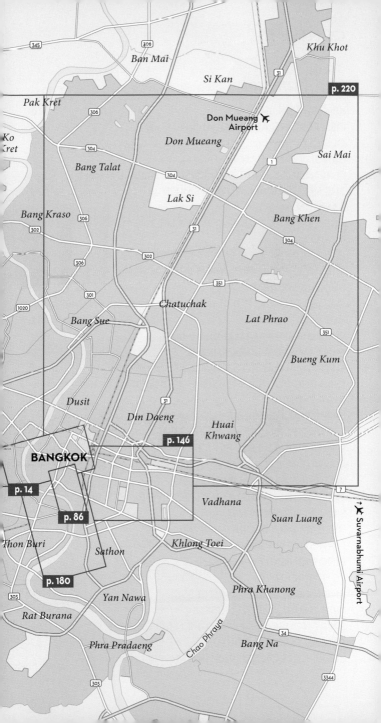

Ban Mai

Khu Khot

Si Kan

p. 220

Pak Kret

Don Mueang
Airport

Ko
Kret

Don Mueang

Sai Mai

Bang Talat

Lak Si

Bang Kraso

Bang Khen

Chatuchak

Lat Phrao

Bang Sue

Bueng Kum

Dusit

Din Daeng

Huai
Khwang

p. 146

BANGKOK

p. 14

p. 86

Vadhana

Suan Luang

Thon Buri

Sathon

Khlong Toei

p. 180

Phra Khanong

Yan Nawa

Rat Burana

Phra Pradaeng

Chao Phraya

Bang Na

Suvarnabhumi Airport

CONTENTS

Old Bangkok

Chinatown

Bangkok West

East Bangkok

CONTENTS

South Bangkok

North Bangkok

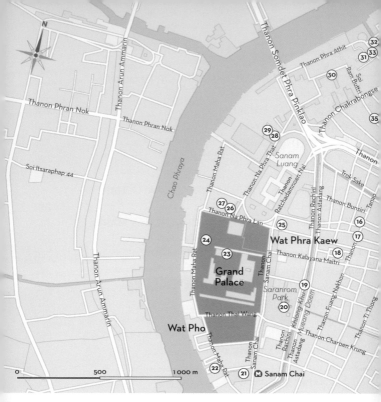

Old Bangkok

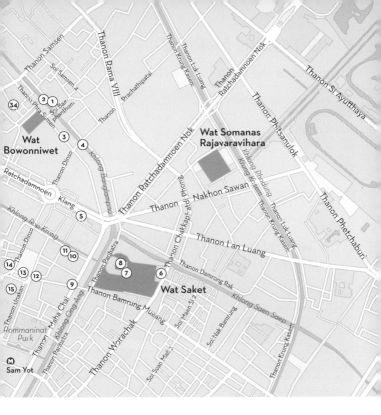

KING TAKSIN SHRINE

Memorial to the forefather of Bangkok

Trok Ban Thom, Phra Nakhon
Daily 7am–5pm

While the popular statue of Taksin the Great (sculpted by Silpa Bhirasri, see p. 66) stands proudly at Wongwian Yai, one of the busiest intersections in Bangkok, there is another very tranquil, and some would say more poignant, place to pay respects to the forefather of Bangkok. Along the peaceful northern bank of Banglamphu Canal (see p. 22), a little-known but very well kept shrine stands in quiet homage to the former king. A statue of the seated Taksin the Great, wearing his distinctive hat, is enclosed within a white building with an ornate façade that is decorated with Chinese lanterns, script and dragons, reflecting his Chinese heritage.

The story of Taksin (1734–1782) is one of historic rise and fall. Born to a Thai mother and a Chinese immigrant father (who ran a gambling monopoly in Ayutthaya), Taksin ascended through the ranks of the army and established a new Siamese capital after the dramatic fall of Ayutthaya in 1767.

Taksin's parents named him Sin, and he spent time as a monk and a trader before he entered royal service. Sin's military prowess was obvious, and by the time he was 30 he was Governor of Tak, an important garrison town in the north-west of Thailand. Three years later, and seven months after Ayutthaya was destroyed by the Burmese, he regained Siam's independence and was crowned King Taksin.

Taksin ruled Siam for 15 years. He was occupied with warfare during much of that time, but also set about building canals and establishing his new capital at Thonburi, where almost a century earlier forts had been built to protect Ayutthaya from ships sailing up the Chao Phraya River. One of those forts, Wichai Prasit, still exists today and, along with the old Thonburi Palace, has become a part of the Royal Thai Navy Headquarters (not open to the public).

The demise of Taksin's reign was unfitting for the man now referred to as King Taksin the Great. In 1782 there was a revolt against the king – army officials claimed that the years of warfare and the pressure of ruling Siam had driven Taksin insane. Taksin agreed to step down (saying he would join a monastery), and his trusted general and long-time friend General Chakri, who was not involved in the revolt, was chosen to ascend the throne.

There was a problem, however: back then it was unheard of for a monarch to abdicate, and a dethroned king was considered a danger to Siam. The only solution, the history books say, was to kill him. Taksin was executed by the method reserved for disgraced royalty – he was hit on the back of the head with a sandalwood club (see p. 110).

With the crowning of General Chakri (posthumously referred to as Rama I) so began the city of Bangkok (see p. 20 and p. 196) and the reign of the Chakri Dynasty, which remains the ruling house of Thailand.

FISH FEEDING AT BANGLAMPHU CANAL

Making merit with the giant catfish

Next to King Taksin Shrine
Trok Ban Thom, Phra Nakhon

The footbridge that arches over Banglamphu Canal (see p. 22) near the King Taksin Shrine (see p. 16) might seem like a tableau of tranquillity, but often the water in the *khlong* (canal) below swirls with the maelstrom of a feeding frenzy. It is as if the *khlong* is boiling as hundreds of catfish (many almost 1 metre long) fight for the bread which has been dropped from above. There are many places around Bangkok where people make offerings of this sort as a way of making merit, but this pretty bridge is perhaps the most spectacular.

Although you are unlikely to see true goliaths here in the *khlong*, the Chao Phraya giant catfish (*Pangasius sanitwongsei*), a member of the shark catfish family, have been known to grow to almost 3 metres long and weigh close to 300 kg. Whether you travel along the river or up the sleepiest *khlongs*, you are likely to see fishermen sitting with their rods, hoping for a bite.

Around fish-feeding spots, however, there will not be a fisherman in sight. It is forbidden to fish close to a temple, or to wherever the faithful make their offerings to the fish. In any case it would be considered bad karma, and few Thais would choose to eat them: "We make offerings to the fish so that they will carry away our bad luck," they explain. "Therefore, if somebody was to eat the fish, he could be cursed with that same luck."

Another (more famous) fish-feeding spot

One of Bangkok's most famous fish-feeding spots is at Nonthaburi Ferry Terminal (in front of the Museum of Nonthaburi, see p. 248). Here, licensed vendors sell huge sacks of brightly coloured fish food, and the fish are in such immense numbers that ducks sometimes walk right across their backs. Visitors are more than welcome to take advantage of an opportunity to make merit too — or simply to feed the fish and make a wish.

"Making merit" explained

Thais believe that acts of merit (*bun* in Thai) in this life will be translated into good karma and a more enlightened existence in the next incarnation. Merit making can take many forms. Rama IV defined real merit as having social value: the wealthy could build monasteries (or, nowadays, schools or hospitals) while the poor might build a bamboo bridge or fix a pothole. Both could give alms. This tradition has become part of Thailand's welfare system with merit-makers donating everything from coffins (see p. 154) to cat food (see p. 80).

OLD CITY WALL

A grand gateway to old Bangkok

365, 10 Phra Sumen Road, Phra Nakhon

Opposite Wat Bowonniwet there is a 40-metre-long wall that looks very out of place on busy Phra Sumen Road. The old white structure, which has a majestic gateway in its centre and is topped with ramparts, marks the boundary of old Bangkok.

Bangkok was founded in 1782 when Rama I established Rattanakosin as the capital of Siam. It became Siam's third capital in just 15 years: when Ayutthaya, which had been the seat of power in the Siamese kingdom for more than four centuries, fell to the Burmese it was so badly destroyed that Taksin the Great, who liberated Siam, moved the capital to Thonburi.

Thonburi lay on the west bank of the Chao Phraya River, which Rama I considered an unsafe location because it was open to attack from the west by the Burmese – so he moved his capital over the river to Bangkok, a small town that was once a thriving trading centre. The reason? The deep, fast-flowing river would protect the vulnerable western border of his new capital.

Rama I erected the city pillar (see p. 64), and then built a series of canals, forts and walls around his new capital. Before long Rattanakosin became an island encircled by the Chao Phraya River and the Khlong Rop Krung ("canal encircling the city", now called Khlong Banglamphu, see p. 22), with a 7.2-km-long wall running along that canal. What is left of the city wall – a 6-metre-high structure with an arched 3-metre-wide doorway in the middle – is what you now see opposite Wat Bowonniwet.

There were 63 gates in the wall, 16 of which were tower gates, like this one. Those that were not tower gates were simple doorways, and all of them, with the exception of Pratu Phi (see p. 32), were protected by blessings and enchantments to keep evil spirits out of the city.

Much of the wall and the 14 forts were built with materials from Taksin's old city walls or salvaged from what was left of Ayutthaya's destroyed forts. Only two of Rama I's forts now remain: Phra Sumen and Mahakan, both of which stand on what is today Phra Sumen Road. Fort Pong Patchamit (see p. 196), on the western bank of the Chao Phraya River, was built at a later stage, when Bangkok expanded during the reign of Rama IV (1851 to 1868).

BANGLAMPHU CANAL

Tracing the edge of old Bangkok

Corner of Phra Athit and Phra Sumen roads, Phra Nakhon

In the morning, as Bangkok's 9.5 million people begin their day, the city's roads fill with traffic, and taxi boats churn up the Chao Phraya River, making criss-crossing waves. Noise intensifies and sidewalks become crowded ... yet along the historic Khlong (Canal) Banglamphu (once, and sometimes still, called Khlong Rop Krung, "canal encircling the city"), the morning lumbers in at a languid pace that invites one to pause and drink in the atmospheric surroundings.

A walk along Khlong Banglamphu also provides the chance to trace Bangkok's city limits as they were in the 1780s, when Rama I created a protective boundary on the east of Rattanakosin (see p. 20). To experience remnants of Bangkok's early days, begin your walk on the

bank of the river at the picturesque Phra Sumen Fort, built to protect this north-western corner of the old city, and then cross to the north side of the canal at Samsen Road. From there it is a very pleasant 1.5 km stroll along the canal to Mahakan Fort and Wat Saket.

More than an escape from the city bustle, an early-morning walk along this *khlong* will give you a peek into city life at a very local level. You will pass a neighbourhood food market, people paying their respects at the King Taksin Shrine (see p. 16), little canal-side coffee stalls, potted gardens, a pretty bridge where people make merit (see p. 19), and all along the way you will see monks collecting alms on their morning rounds (see p. 82).

Bangkok: Venice of the East

Bangkok, now one of the world's fastest-sinking cities, lies on the Chao Phraya delta. When the city was founded, the area was predominantly swampland, and Rama I's palace, temples and housing for the elite were the only buildings on dry land. Bangkok developed around an intricate network of *khlongs* built to drain and channel the natural flow of water in the area, and well into the 19th century almost all structures for commoners existed on, rather than beside, the water. It was only in 1864 – 82 years after Bangkok was founded – that Charoen Krung Road, the first public road suitable for horse-drawn carriages, was opened.

Bangkok's raft houses were outlawed in 1900 and stilt houses no longer exist along Khlong Banglamphu, but you can see some at Bang Kraso (see p. 250) if you take a longtail boat tour of the *khlongs* on the Thonburi side of the river (the boats leave from Phra Athit pier).

"THE INSIDE" AT RATTANAKOSIN EXHIBITION HALL

A rare glimpse into the Grand Palace's "forbidden city"

Rattanakosin Exhibition Hall
100 Ratchadamnoen Klang Avenue, Phra Nakhon
nitasrattanakosin.com
Tuesday to Sunday 10am–5pm; tours start every 20 minutes (you are not allowed to visit the exhibitions on your own)

The Inner Court Complex, often known as "The Inside", was a closed community of about 3,000 women who were the wives, consorts, concubines and daughters of the king, as well as their entourages of female servants.

Located to the south of the Grand Palace (behind Chakri Maha Prasat Throne Hall, see p. 60), it is inaccessible to outsiders even today, but the Prestige of the Kingdom Room at the Rattanakosin Exhibition Hall gives a rare insight into life behind these walls. Here, there are scenes that depict the activities that took place in The Inside in the 1800s, and informative texts on the strict regulations, lifestyle, fashion, traditions and etiquette of this shielded place.

Traditionally the king's residence and gardens were located in The Inside. Apart from the king and his young sons, no men were allowed, but if a physician needed to enter, for example, he would be supervised by the *khlon*, the female security guards of this inner court.

Rattanakosin Exhibition Hall is a good place to learn about early Bangkok as it sheds light on the cultural legacies of the Rattanakosin Era (from 1782). Displays show how neighbourhoods were set up according to trades and crafts, and reveal the development of the city, the evolution of the architectural styles, and the characteristics of various art forms, including murals and puppets.

There are two different two-hour guided tours of the exhibitions. One focuses on the traditions, communities and Bangkokian way of life, while the other concentrates on the development of the city. Both are interesting and well worth taking.

Ratchadamnoen Klang: inspired by Paris' Avenue des Champs-Élysées

Ratchadamnoen is a wide boulevard that leads from Dusit Royal Palace to the Grand Palace. The construction of this road began in 1899 during the reign of Rama V, the first Thai king to visit Europe. It is said that his inspiration for Ratchadamnoen was Paris' Avenue des Champs-Élysées. Rama V died in 1910, but in 1937 when the grand buildings in the middle section of the road (Ratchadamnoen Klang, where the Rattanakosin Exhibition Hall stands) were designed, the architectural style was in keeping with Rama V's vision, and many buildings reflect the influence of Western design principles. "Eastern Classical" was the popular architectural style at that time, which had an emphasis on symmetry, proportion and balance.

THE HELL MURALS AT WAT SAKET ⑥

The astounding secret corners of a popular temple

Wat Saket
344 Thanon Chakkraphatdi Phong, Pom Prap Sattru Phai
Daily 7.30am–7pm

W at Saket's Golden Mount receives a fair number of visitors, but there still are a few secret spots around this temple. You will see one of the most remarkable of these if you bypass the Golden Mount altogether and walk about 350 metres to the rarely visited eastern edge of the temple complex.

There you will find the majestic bodhi tree that, legend has it, was a seedling taken from a tree which itself was grown from a cutting of the tree under which Buddha was sitting when he attained enlightenment, almost 2,500 years ago.

From the heavenly shade of the bodhi tree, walk a few metres into the neighbouring "Consecrated Convocation Hall". The interior of the entire hall is covered with spectacular murals: dramatic battle scenes depicting bearded Arab warriors and Portuguese mercenaries in tricorn hats, and soldiers and demons grapple desperately with tigers and buffalos. These images are intriguing enough to be worth a visit in their own right … but head to the back of the room behind the 2-metre-high gilded Buddha and things become even more bizarre.

Despite the crowds climbing the Golden Mount, few people (even among the guides) seem to be aware of the diabolical and very graphic scenes shown here – a series of images that could have offered inspiration to Hieronymus Bosch. The murals depict various levels of Naraka, the term from Buddhist cosmology that is best translated as "hell". The murals are particularly well executed, but the imagery presents a disturbing imagining of the karma that might await evildoers.

Hapless beings sit tongue-tied and hogtied while their mouths are sewn up. Nearby, tongues are being pulled out with long pliers. Those undergoing a simple beheading seem almost blessed in comparison with one particularly bemused-looking man who is having his head sawn in half from the top down. The crimes they have committed can only be imagined, particularly when you realise that unlike Christian hell, one is reborn into a Naraka as a result of karma, and the duration of time here is predetermined (but is said to be hundreds of millions of years).

There are a few temples in Bangkok with murals depicting Naraka, and a modern example can be seen just inches from an effigy of David Beckham, at Wat Pariwat (see p. 214). For more on other aspects of the Golden Mount's ghoulish past, see p. 30.

BAMIYAN MUSEUM

⑦

Palm leaf manuscripts dating back over 1,500 years

Wat Saket
344 Thanon Chakkraphatdi Phong, Pom Prap Sattru Phai
Daily 7.30am–7pm

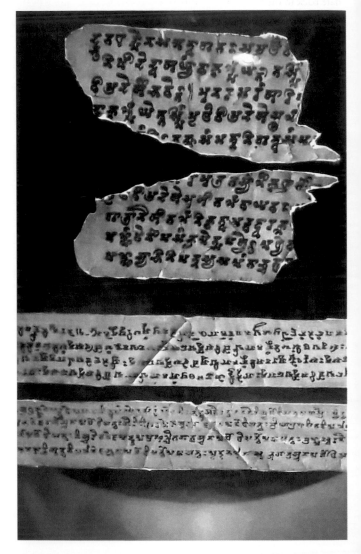

Tucked into the grotto on the south-eastern flank of the Golden Mount, there is a museum that houses a collection of artefacts originally from Afghanistan's Bamiyan Valley, which was once a prominent centre of Buddhism along the famed Silk Road.

The palm-leaf fragments of the Bodhisattvapitaka Sutra scriptures are the pride of the Bamiyan Museum's collection. These scriptures date back to the 5th or 6th century, and are among the oldest Buddhist scriptures in the world. They were donated by Norwegian manuscript collector Dr Martin Schøyen, and had been prized artefacts in his collection of more than 20,000 manuscripts which spanned more than 5,000 years of human culture.

Manuscripts were removed from the Bamiyan Valley in the late 1990s for safe-keeping and were held in the British Museum and the Schøyen Collection before some were relocated to Bangkok.

"I'm proud to have played a part in preserving these important parts of Buddhist scripture so that they can now be studied by scholars, and venerated by believers half a world away from where they rested for centuries, but where they came under threat of destruction", said Schøyen when he presented the fragments to the museum in 2010.

A replica of one of the Bamiyan Buddhas

The museum also has a replica of one of the famous Bamiyan Buddhas. The original Buddha images were carved into the cliffs and caves in the Bamiyan Valley about 1,500 years ago and the largest, which stood at 55 metres tall, was considered the world's largest rock-carved Buddha. In March 2001, two of the Bamiyan Buddhas, Afghanistan's major tourist attractions, were dynamited and destroyed by the Taliban.

VULTURE SCULPTURE
AT WAT SAKET

A gruesome tableau of one of Bangkok's most horrific periods

Wat Saket, 344 Thanon Chakkraphatdi Phong, Pom Prap Sattru Phai
Daily 7.30am–7pm

On the northern flank of Wat Saket (also known as the Golden Mount) there is a very lifelike tableau showing a group of bystanders watching vultures feast on a corpse. This gruesome sculpture depicts what was a common scene here in the second half of the 1800s, when cholera epidemics killed many of Bangkok's inhabitants and vultures fed on the corpses awaiting cremation.

The tradition was that except for the bodies of royals, cremations could not take place within the walls of the city. At that time, because Wat Saket was just beyond the walls, corpses were transported there. Over the 60 years that the periodic cholera epidemics took place – and particularly in 1849 when an epidemic killed one tenth of the city's population – Wat Saket became famous for its bickering flocks of vultures. One unexpected result of the great pile of corpses and feathered diners was that some celebrated monks were drawn to this temple by the opportunity to meditate over the "impermanence of existence".

The Scandinavian explorer and writer Carl Bock survived a cholera epidemic here in 1881, and his excellent book *Temples and Elephants*, published three years later, remains one of the best travelogues on old Siam. At the time of his visit, as many as 120 bodies were arriving at Wat Saket via the Ghost Gate (see p. 32) in a single day. The usual process of cremation could not keep pace with the mortality rate and other means had to be found: Bock described the ghastly spectacle of a pauper's corpse being prepared for the vultures by "a temple butcher with a huge knife who cut the body open, with a long slash down the stomach … the flesh from the thighs, legs and arms was then cut off, and the chest opened".

An old Bangkok tradition, perhaps dating back to these times, holds that you should always refer to a vulture in the most respectful terms if you want to avoid bad luck. The ideal compliment goes something along the lines of *chao phya hong thong*, "most noble golden swan".

What's in a name?

Macabre as the vulture story is, Wat Saket has a gentler side: the temple's name translates as "wash hair". General Chakri stopped here to undertake ceremonial bathing on his return from Laos with the Emerald Buddha. After the general was crowned king of Siam (Rama I), the temple was renamed Wat Saket Ratcha Wora Mahana Wihan.

PRATU PHI

Bangkok's feared "Ghost Gate"

Samran Rat Junction, Phra Nakhon

Where Bamrung Mueang Road – historically one of Bangkok's most important trading thoroughfares – crosses Sommot Amonmak Bridge, it passes through a junction that is still known to old-timers as Pratu Phi (Ghost Gate). The gate itself, once part of the old city walls (see p. 20), has long gone but many say that the junction is still haunted by its dark history.

Throughout the 1800s, by official decree, corpses could only be taken out of the city through the gateway that was closest to Wat Saket. Thousands of corpses passed through this Ghost Gate on their way to cremation, burial or dismemberment (see p. 30). At one time it was one of 63 gates in the old city walls, but the Ghost Gate alone had the dubious distinction of being the only one that was left unprotected by blessings and enchantments ... how else would the ghosts of the deceased be able to pass *out* of the city?

As you stand at the junction, turn towards the north-western corner and you will see Bangkok's first pawnshop (in operation for more than 150 years), then turn directly to the west and you will be staring at the great looming shape that citizens will tell you is often mistaken for a ghost. The type of ghost known as *pret* is said to be extremely tall and thin ... so tall and thin, in fact, that some people have claimed that the nocturnal sightings of *pret* which happen from time to time in this area might be explained by the 21.15-metre-high Giant Swing at the end of the street.

In Wat Suthat Thepwararam (see p. 44) a mural depicts a *pret*, and in his book about novice monks titled *Little Angels* (Random House, 2005), Phra Peter Pannapadipo recounts the story of a young monk who asked to be transferred to another monastery after he saw a *pret*. The monk described it as being about 20 feet tall with a potbelly, very long fingernails and tangled white hair. A 2003 horror drama series called *Pret Wat Satat* made the ghost even more famous ... although in general the Ghost Gate's giant spectre seems to prefer to maintain a low profile.

When a place (or a person) seems to have had more than its fair share of misfortune, a common Thai remedy is often simply to rename it. In just such a mood of spiritual whitewashing, Pratu Phi is now officially known as Samran Rat (Happy Citizen).

BHIKKHUNI IMAGES
AT WAT THEPTHIDARAM

Unique statues that depict female Buddhist monks

Wat Thepthidaram Woraviharn, 70 Mahachai Road, Phra Nakhon
watthepthidaramqr.com
Daily 7.30am–6pm

The *viharn* (sermon hall) in a Thai Buddhist temple is a building that contains a collection of Buddha images, but the one at Wat Thepthidaram is unlike any other in Thailand, as it houses beautiful statues of 52 female Buddhist monks. With them is an image of Mahapajapati Gotami, the first *bhikkhuni* (female Buddhist monk), who was Buddha's aunt and stepmother. These statues are set around a Buddha image and each one is in a different pose.

Rama III built the temple in 1836 to honour Princess Wilat, his favourite daughter. The full name of the temple is Wat Thepthidaram Woraviharn – "Noble Temple of the Heavenly Angel" – and throughout the temple complex women are celebrated. In the same hall as the *bhikkhuni* images, a Chinese phoenix – a symbol of femininity – is painted on the wall, and stone statues of women stand in the gardens.

According to Thai art historian Dr Pattaratorn Chirapravati, the *bhikkhuni* images "reflect the importance of women in monastic literature and the increasing role of female practitioners in Bangkok in the 1830s". By 1928, however, religious and secular laws forbidding the ordination of women were passed. Today, Thailand's Buddhist clergy still does not acknowledge women who want to become monks, so those who wish to be ordained must travel abroad.

There are some 300,000 monks in Thailand, and only about 100 *bhikkhuni*. Former academic Dr Chatsumarn Kabilsingh was the first modern Thai woman to receive full ordination, and was ordained in Sri Lanka in 2001. Now known as Venerable Dhammananda, she is the Abbess of Songdhammakalyani, an all-women monastery (founded by her mother) in Nakhon Pathom, an hour east of Bangkok.

Princess Wilat: a highly respected royal

Krom Muen Absonsudathep (1811–1845), or Princess Wilat, was the third daughter of Rama III. She was an indispensable member of the king's court, overseeing the palace expenses and running the administration of various offices in The Inside (see p. 24). Princess Wilat was a long-time patron of the great poet Sunthorn Phu (see p. 36), and it was she who encouraged him, while he was a monk, to continue to write his epics, and to teach literature and poetry. Portraits of Princess Wilat and Rama III hang in the *ubosot* (the temple's chapel).

SUNTHORN PHU MUSEUM

The home of Thailand's greatest poet

Wat Thepthidaram
70 Mahachai Road, Phra Nakon
watthepthidaramqr.com
Daily 9am–5pm

Sunthorn Phu (1786–1855) is regarded as Thailand's greatest poet. He once lived at Wat Thepthidaram, where a small but informative museum commemorates the work of the man whose verse and prose are still taught in schools and universities across Thailand. At the museum, monks guide visitors through the rooms in which the old poet lived,

and where relics of his life and work are now displayed (the fun and quirky interactive features are a particular highlight, and the photos the monks take of you "interacting" with a hologram of the poet make for memorable souvenirs).

Many of Sunthorn Phu's most important works include poems about journeys. *Nirat Mueang Klaeng* is about a journey to Rayong province, and his epic *Phra Aphai Mani*, which Sunthorn Phu began while in prison, follows a prince on his romantic adventures around Thailand.

Sunthorn Phu's life followed a pattern of highs and lows. During the reign of Rama I, he worked at the Grand Palace as a clerk. There, he fell in love with a woman named Jun, but their relationship was forbidden because she was related to the royal family (some sources say the poet was subsequently jailed). Once their romance was pardoned, the couple married, but soon divorced – the poet had turned to alcohol, and Jun left him. Sunthorn Phu married again twice, but admitted that the woman he had loved the most was Jun.

Sunthorn Phu was appointed royal poet during the reign of Rama II. He rose to prominence composing poetry for the king who, delighted with the poet's work, granted him the noble title *Khun*. However, Sunthorn Phu was stripped of this title during the reign of Rama III, when he publicly corrected one of the king's poems.

Sunthorn Phu left the royal courts in disgrace, and became a vagabond who sold poems to earn a living. He eventually turned to the monkhood and was ordained at Wat Thepthidaram, where he came under the patronage of Princess Wilat (see p. 35), who knew and enjoyed his poems.

Back in favour with the royal family, Sunthorn Phu was made Head of Scribes. During the reign of Rama IV he was granted the noble title *Phra*, and appointed Director of Royal Scribes. He retired from the palace at the age of 70, and died a decade later.

The royal vocabulary

Thai people use a vocabulary called Rachasap when speaking to or about a member of the Thai royal family. Some words are the same as "ordinary" Thai, but prefixes or suffixes are added or changed, while others stem from the Khmer language. Rachasap developed during the Sukhothai period (about 700 years ago), when Thailand's culture was strongly influenced by the Khmer Empire.

BUDDHA WORKSHOPS

Where oversized Buddha images are completed

177 Bamrung Mueang Road (corner of Siri Phong Road)
Samran Rat, Phra Nakhon
Daily 8am–5pm

Even in a place that seems so unnaturally super-sized – where a plaque displays the longest city name in the world (see next page), and the Giant Swing stands – the huge Buddha images lining the pavement of Siri Phong Road come as a surprise. For generations, this quarter has been producing oversized statues, and it is worth a visit for anyone curious about the birthplace of some of the city's most astounding Buddha images.

In 1881 Scandinavian writer Carl Bock described this same row of shops in his book *Temples and Elephants*: "The sale of these idols must be one of the most profitable industries in Bangkok," he wrote. "The sale is constant and increasing, and the mere work of gilding and re-gilding the most expensive figures never ceases." In those days most of the figures were made of wood and Bock lamented that "the carefully wrought bronze castings are becoming more and more rare".

Bronze and copper are again the norm, with hardwood sculptures now extremely rare. Today these artefacts are mostly produced in the suburbs, but many are completed, polished and coated with gold colouring in the small workshops found down an alley on the corner of Bamrung Mueang and Siri Phong Roads.

The Buddha statues on the sidewalk, some around 3 metres tall, can take four months to make. They are a startling sight and, with a price tag of over US$18,000, you would imagine that they would represent a serious purchase for anyone. "Buddha is *not* for decoration," Jim Phandthong emphasises as he stands in the workshop that his grandfather started more than 50 years ago. "I always confirm that my statues are to be used for serious purposes."

The road where gold leaf was made

The most expensive statues sold in this area are still coated with real gold leaf – *bai lan* – which used to be prepared in nearby Thanon Ti Thong (Goldsmith Road). The gold was laid between buffalo hide pads and pounded with mallets. When it was warmed, it would be spread into thin sheets that could be cut into squares. Today Thanon Ti Thong is better known for producing gold and silver insignia and you will see bureaucrats here purchasing decorations for their uniforms.

THE 168-CHARACTER PLAQUE OF BANGKOK'S NAME

The world's longest city name

Lan Khon Mueang
Bamrung Mueang Road, Phra Nakhon

Along the edge of Bamrung Mueang Road, as it sweeps between City Hall and the famous Giant Swing, there is a long – very long – plaque that displays Bangkok's full name in Thai. The name is so long that if you picked up the 16-metre-long plaque and turned it around, it would effectively barricade the entire six-lane avenue of Bamrung Mueang.

The name "Bangkok" might be just two brief syllables in English, but in Thai the city officially has the longest name of any city on the planet. In Thai script – กรุงเทพมหานคร อมรรัตนโกสินทร์ มหินทรายุธยามหาดิลก ภพนพรัตน์ ราชธานีบุรีรมย์ อุดมราชนิเวศน์ มหาสถาน อมรพิมาน อวตารสถิต สักกะทัตติยะ วิษณุกรรมประสิทธิ์ – the city's full name is an incredible 168 characters long.

Fortunately, it is not considered disrespectful to abbreviate the name of the Thai capital, and "Krung Thep Maha Nakhon Amon Rattanakosin Mahinthrayutthhaya Maha Dilokphop Noppharat Ratchathani Burirom Udom Ratchaniwet Maha Sathan Amon Phiman Awatan Sathit Sakkathattiya Witsanukam Prasit" is usually referred to in Thai simply as Krung Thep.

According to an English sign beside the plaque, the full name translates as "The City That Is Very Large Like The City Of Angels; Houses The Sacred Emerald Buddha; Has Prosperity And Stable Beauty; Is Abundant With The Pleasant Nine Gems; Has Numerous Royal Grand Palaces; And Is A Fairy Abode Created On The Earth By Thao Sakka Thewarat Witsanukam For The Incarnated Divinities".

It is doubtful whether experts will ever agree on the origin of the name "Bangkok". Some claim that it may have derived from "Bang Khaek", referring to the city's large Muslim (Khaek) population. Others say that "Bang Gawk" was a place with lots of olive trees (although it is doubtful that there was ever a time when either olives or Muslims were sufficiently numerous to warrant naming the city after them). Others say it may have come from "Bang Ko" (a house or village on an island) or "Bang Makok" (the village of wild plums).

With the Thai language being such a fluid and tonal one, you can almost take your pick. Or, if you prefer, just call it "City of Angels".

By comparison the famous Welsh town of Llanfairpwllgwyngyll-gogerychwyrndrobwllllantysiliogogogoch is a relative paragon of brevity with a mere 58 characters.

DHEVASATHAN

The centre of Hinduism in Thailand

268 Dinso Road, Phra Nakhon
Daily 9am–6pm

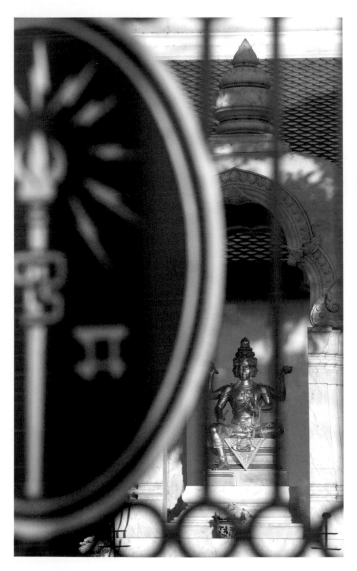

Serene Dhevasathan, known as the "Shrine of the Gods of the Capital City", provides insights into an unexpected aspect of religion in the world's second largest Buddhist country. The temple is the centre of Hinduism and Brahmanism in Thailand, and throughout the year, Brahmin priests perform many important royal and religious ceremonies for the Thai monarchy.

More than one thousand years ago, the kings of Siam invited Brahmin priests from India to preside over coronations in the hope that they would thus rise in status to be equal to the might of the kings of India. To this day, Dhevasathan remains the official home of Thailand's Court Brahmins, descendants of an ancient lineage of priests from Tamil Nadu. The traditional belief was that these priests held the key to heaven, and that their chanting opened the divine gates so that the gods could descend to Earth.

The first thing you will see when you enter the ornate gates of Dhevasathan, which was built by Rama I in 1784, is a gilded statue of the four-faced god Brahma. Legend has it that Brahma once became so infatuated with a beautiful goddess he had created that he grew five heads so as to never lose sight of her. Shiva, angry that Brahma was so obsessed with one of his own creations, then chopped off the top head. The four remaining heads are said to represent kindness, sympathy, mercy and impartiality.

Behind this pavilion there are three small temples: one is dedicated to Shiva (the destroyer), one to Ganesha (featuring the oldest effigy of the elephant-headed god in Thailand, dating from the 5th century) and one to Vishnu (the preserver).

PHRA BUDDHA SETHAMUNI IMAGE

Cast in 1839 from confiscated opium boxes

Wat Suthat Thepwararam
146 Bamrung Mueang Road, Phra Nakhon
Daily 8am–6pm
Dress code: conservative. It is best to wear long trousers or a skirt below the knee, shirts or tops with a respectable neckline and sleeves that reach the elbow or below. Ripped jeans, shorts, short skirts and tight trousers, including leggings, may not be worn. Shoulders must not be showing. See-through clothes must not be worn.

Wat Suthat, which was consecrated in 1807, is one of the most impressive but overlooked temples in the city. It was designed to represent the centre of the universe according to Thai Buddhist cosmology, and it took 40 years to complete the complex, which covers an area the size of six soccer fields. The scale of this temple is truly spectacular, and yet this grand space contains veiled objects and stories that are rarely told.

The ashes of Rama VIII are buried under the Buddha image at Wat Suthat and in the temple's courtyard you will see a statue of that king, the older brother of Thailand's much-loved Rama IX (who was the world's longest reigning monarch, holding the throne for 70 years, 126 days).

One of the hidden gems at Wat Suthat – which not even regular worshippers are aware of – is the unique Buddha image housed in the temple's second *viharn* (sermon hall). Phra Buddha Sethamuni, as it is known, was cast in 1839 from confiscated opium boxes. The opium trade was illegal at that time – Rama III had introduced the death penalty for major opium traffickers – and the tin and lead opium cannisters used to create this Buddha had been seized from drug lords. Rama III had hoped that by recasting them as a Buddha image, something good would come from something fundamentally evil.

The tragic story of Rama VIII

The story of Rama VIII, the king who was never crowned, is a tragic one. Prince Ananda Mahidol was born in 1925 in Germany, where his parents (see p. 193) were studying at the time. The prince was nine years old and at school in Switzerland when his uncle, Rama VII (who was childless), abdicated and Mahidol was proclaimed Thailand's next king. As the prince was so young, two regents were appointed while he continued his studies in Switzerland. He returned to Bangkok for a visit in 1946, but four days before he was due to return to Switzerland to complete his doctoral degree in law, Rama VIII was found shot dead in his bed. The king's secretary and two pages were convicted of murder, but there has always been much controversy surrounding his death.

SAN CHAOPHO SUEA SHRINE

The Tiger God with a taste for bacon and eggs

468 Tanao Road, Phra Nakhon
Daily 6am–5pm

nown locally as the "Tiger God Shrine", San Chaopho Suea Shrine is dedicated to Xuanwu, a warrior-god so fierce that he has tigers for servants. The two stone tigers at the main entrance gave the shrine its name.

In Thailand, every deity seems to have their preferred offerings, and if you arrive at this Taoist joss house in the morning, you are sure to get the impression that the Tiger God enjoys nothing more than bacon and eggs for breakfast. Around dawn a row of stalls begins to appear outside the shrine, with parasols opening like giant sunflowers. Each stall is heaped with polystyrene trays bearing rice, an egg and a thick rasher of pork.

There are also effigies of other Taoist deities here: Guan Yu (God of Honesty), Caishen (God of Fortune), Sun Wukong (Magic Monkey) and Mazu (Goddess of the Sea, see p. 194). Apart from the proffered pork and eggs, you will see worshippers pouring endless bottles of cooking oil into giant burners, and there are large bunches of incense candles and gigantic red candles sold by the metre. Couples who are hoping for a child will often come here to offer little sugar tigers in the hope that fertility will be bestowed upon them.

You have to wonder how the shrine can withstand such daily fire-hazards, but although large fires have periodically destroyed much of the quarter (see p. 48), the Tiger God Shrine has always remained unharmed – thus, of course, enhancing its mystic power in the eyes of devotees.

One legend has it that the original tiger was a man-eater that lived in the area when the shrine was founded in 1834, but the shrine's original site was slightly farther east on Bamrung Mueang Road, and it is extremely doubtful there were any tigers left in the area by then.

In 1870, when plans were made to relocate the shrine to its current position to make way for a row of crown-owned shophouses, a religious leader prophesied that anyone attempting to move it would incur the wrath of the gods. Rama V promptly responded by prophesying that anyone making pro-phesies that stood in the way of royal progress would incur the wrath of the king... and the holy man agreed that the gods would, after all, doubtless understand the need for moving the shrine.

GATE OF PHRAENG SANPHASAT

An Art Nouveau treasure

Phraeng Sanphasat Road
Phra Nakhon

The beautiful gateway at the junction of Phraeng Sanphasat and Thanon Tanao is the type which you are more likely to see in Paris or Prague than in downtown Bangkok. But then this neighbourhood, traditionally one of Bangkok's most cosmopolitan areas, was planned by Rama V after he returned from Europe. Sam Phraeng quarter – named after its junction of three roads (each of which was named after one of Rama IV's sons, who lived here) – was once one of the most sought-after residential areas for those with a yearning for a Western city lifestyle.

The palace of Prince Sanphasat Suphakij, who was head of the Military Engineers Corps during the reigns of Rama V (1868 to 1910) and Rama VI (1910 to 1925), must have been a masterpiece of European-style architecture when it was constructed in 1906. It is not clear who the architect was – it may have been an exercise in Art Nouveau by the Italian architect Mario Tamagno or the German architect Karl Döhring, both of whom were working in Bangkok at that time. When the prince died in 1919, his palace was destroyed to make way for shophouses, and this gateway is all that remains of the palace.

The prince was also responsible for the royal goldsmiths, and around 1890 a German man by the name of Grählert became jeweller to the king. Many of his workers and suppliers lived in this quarter, especially in Trok Chang Thong (still known as "alley of the gold workers"). In fact, the quarter became so synonymous with the precious metal that it was common to see people panning for gold in nearby canals, and gold dust and scraps were discovered under floorboards during house renovations even decades later. One resident apparently flooded the ground underneath his house (which had been owned by a goldsmith) and used the 45 grams of gold he found to make an amulet.

The Gate of Phraeng Sanphasat was badly damaged in a fire in 1967, and nine years later the Fine Arts Department was tasked with renovating the arch, which now stands as an unexpected sight in what remains a charming residential area. It is said that whenever there was a fire here, people would come from all over the city to prospect for gold among the ashes and rubble. Perhaps it is not coincidental that the quarter has had more than its share of fires over the years.

PHRAENG PHUTHON NEIGHBOURHOOD

A cityscape from the late 1800s

Phraeng Phuthon Road, Phra Nakhon

There is an area between the Gate of Phraeng Sanphasat (see p. 48) and Khlong Khu Mueang Doem (see p. 52) that contains beautifully preserved examples of Bangkok's cityscape in the late 1800s. This area is where three princes, the sons of Rama IV (1868 to 1910), built their palaces, and it was where new roads and shophouses were built as Bangkok flourished during the reign of Rama V.

Just off Bamrung Mueang Road is the tiny neighbourhood of Phraeng Phuthon. The quiet street, which circles a small park and a clinic, is lined with Straits Settlement-style shophouses that were so popular at the turn of the 20th century. By the 1980s, however, the buildings and neighbourhood had fallen into serious decline and the community banded together to improve their quarter. The buildings are all now painted a cream colour, with teal and green shutters on the windows and doors, and when stepping into this square, void of high-rise buildings, one gets a real sense of old Bangkok.

Enhancing this feeling of stepping back in time are the vintage cars you will see parked unceremoniously on the street. Keep an eye out for them, and then look carefully at the shophouses nearby. One has a small sign outside that reads "Antique Car Coffee" – go in and have a look (and a coffee). This "coffee shop" is actually an old garage called Vichien, and a handful of tables have been placed where there is space inside. Vintage cars – including a few old Austins – and a collection of car parts are still crammed into the garage, which may once have been Bangkok's first Driver's Licence Bureau (which was located in this neighbourhood). The first cars arrived in Bangkok around 1900, and the city's first drivers would have had to drive around the park opposite the garage in order to prove their proficiency.

Phraeng Phuthon's preserved double-storey shophouses – commercial use below, residential above – are acquiring a reputation for their array of delicious food. Look out for a small shop called Nuttaporn, which has been making and serving Thai-style ice cream (which is rolled on an iced pan) for more than six decades. According to the family-run business, they supply the Grand Palace with their ice cream.

PIG MEMORIAL

The statue of a pig, dedicated to a queen

Rachini Alley (along Khlong Khu Mueang Doem, near Pi Kun Bridge)
Phra Nakhon

Alongside one of Bangkok's oldest canals, atop a small tower of white rocks, stands the statue of a pig, partly covered in gold leaf (see p. 38) and draped with strings of plastic pearls. Garlands of marigolds and jasmine buds hang off its nose, and lengths of coloured fabric are wrapped around its base. In the "cave" beneath the pig, still more offerings are made: there are plastic roses and figurines of dancers, servants and animals, and an image of Phra Mae Thoranee, the earth goddess.

This memorial was erected in 1913 to honour Queen Saowabha (see p. 55 and p. 220), a wife of Rama V, on her 50th birthday, because she was born in the Year of the Pig.

Centuries ago, the Thais adopted China's lunisolar calendar, which runs in cycles of 12 years. Each year is named after an animal, and each year has its own element and guardian spirit. Someone born in the Year of the Pig, for example, will have water as their element, and their guardian spirit is a female deity who lives under lotus plants. The year in which one is born is particularly important to Thai people, who believe their horoscopes influence everything from personality traits to health, relationships, lucky numbers and even auspicious directions.

While it is commonly known as the Pig Memorial, the statue does have another name, Sahachat Memorial – "the memorial of those who were born in the same year". It was commissioned by three members of the royal family who were born in the same year as the queen. One of the donors, Prince Narissara Nuwattiwong (see p. 231), designed the monument.

The pillars of Saphan Mu Bridge

The Pig Memorial stands alongside Khlong Khu Mueang Doem (Old City Moat), which was built in the 1770s during the reign of King Taksin. Spanning the canal adjacent to the Pig Memorial is a pretty, white pedestrian bridge that was also built to honour Queen Saowabha. In 1911 she turned 48 – a particularly auspicious birthday because it marked her fourth 12-year cycle, which also fell in the Year of the Pig. The bridge has four decorative pillars that represent a birthday candle for each of the four cycles. The bridge had no name when it was built, and it was only after the Pig Memorial was built that it became known as Saphan Mu (Pig Bridge) and Saphan Pi Kun (Year of the Pig Bridge).

A queen who drowned because at that time, no one apart from the king was allowed to touch a queen

Saranrom Park
Between the intersection of New Road and Rajini Road
Phra Nakhon
Daily 4.30am–9pm

S aranrom Park, one of the prettiest public spaces in Bangkok, has a monument with a sad story – it is dedicated to the memory of Queen Sunanta (1860–1881) and Princess Kannabhorn, who both drowned in 1881.

The pregnant queen, a favourite wife of Rama V, was on a boat with her two-year-old daughter when it capsized. At that time, no one apart from the king was allowed to touch a queen, and so, although there were people around who could have saved her, no one did. The punishment for touching a queen was death.

An inscription on the marble memorial reads: "To the beloved memory of her late and lamented Majesty, Sunanta-Kumariratana, Queen Consort, who was wont to spend her most pleasant and happiest hours in this garden amidst those loving ones and dearest to her. This memorial was erected by Chulalongkorn Rex, her bereaved husband, whose suffering from so cruel an endurance through those trying hours made death seem so near yet so preferable".

The ponds and shade in Saranrom Park offer respite from the city's relentless heat, and the manicured lawns provide a tranquil space for friends and families to gather.

Queens with a cause

Rama V had 92 wives, as polygamy was the norm in Siam. To secure business and familial relationships young noblewomen would be presented to Siamese kings, and it was the custom for them to be accepted as minor wives. To keep royal blood pure for succession, some kings married their half-sisters: Queen Sunanta and her two younger sisters, Queen Sawang (1862–1955) and Queen Saowabha (1864–1919) were the half-sisters and wives of Rama V.

Queens Sawang and Saowabha, both very generous women, remained close friends throughout their lives, and when Queen Saowabha (the Supreme Queen, see p. 53 and p. 220) passed away, her younger sister continued her work. Queen Saowabha founded the Thai Red Cross Society, a school for midwives and six schools for girls. She also paid for many students to study abroad. Queen Sawang gave scholarships for girls to study nursing in the USA, and one recipient married the queen's son, and went on to become the mother of two Thai kings (see p. 192). Queen Saowabha was the mother of Rama VI and Rama VII. Queen Sawang was the grandmother of Rama VIII and Rama IX.

LUK THEP DOLL AT MUSEUM SIAM

Dolls that bring their owners luck and protection

Thai Beliefs Room
Museum Siam
4 Sanam Chai Road
Phra Nakhon
museumsiam.org
Tuesday to Sunday 10am–6pm

A chubby-cheeked doll wearing a polka-dot dress sits on a shelf in the Museum Siam. She is easily overlooked – after all, she is "just" a doll surrounded by more interesting things, like shiny statues of goddesses, glitzy costumes and a fortune-telling slot machine. But do not walk past – pause here, then look above her head.

The sinister-looking object above her is a foetus-doll, known as *kuman thong* (little golden boy). It is a precursor to the doll in the polka dot dress, which is called a *luk thep* (child angel). By 2016 *luk thep* dolls were so popular that Thai Smile Airways instructed staff to sell seats for the dolls, and also to ensure that they were buckled up and served meals, just as regular children would be.

Why the fixation with the dolls' wellbeing? After they have been through a specific ritual or ceremony, it is believed that the dolls will contain a spirit that will, if the owner treats them well, bring the owner good luck, prosperity and protection. Although 94 percent of Thai people are Buddhist, many also hold the animist beliefs that existed here long before Buddhism arrived in the region, and a belief in spirits is deep-rooted in Thai culture.

The *kuman thong* stems from an old folk tale retold in the Thai epic poem *Khun Chang Khun Phaen* (the poet Sunthorn Phu – see p. 36 – contributed to one version of this epic). The story tells of two soldiers who lived during the Ayutthaya Era. One soldier, Khun Paen, was protected from enemy spirits by his own band of spirits, and at one point he was joined by the particularly powerful spirit from the foetus of his unborn son. That spirit was called Kuman Thong. In the past *kuman thong* were foetuses that had been dry roasted (usually in a ceremony that took place before dawn), painted with lacquer and then covered with gold leaf.

Luk thep have a more appealing creation: the lifelike dolls are made from plastic. They originated in 2012 when a Bangkokian woman known as Mama Ning placed amulets on a doll, and it "awakened". Her life started to improve. Within a few years the word had spread, and by 2015 Thai celebrities were posting photographs of their dolls on social media, attributing their luck and success to their *luk thep*. Owners often consider them human, and carry their dolls around malls, as they would a young child.

WHITE MOUSE RACING MEMORABILIA

Mementos from Thailand's motor-racing heroes

White Mouse Bar & Café
396 Maharaj Road
Phra Nakhon
facebook.com/whitemousecafe
Daily 10am–6pm

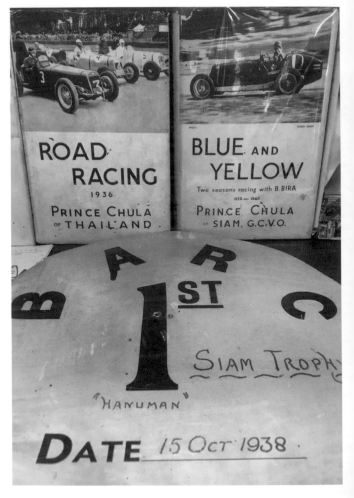

A blue sign with a white mouse hangs outside a small café on the banks of the Chao Phraya River. It is unlikely that passers-by could ever imagine what memorabilia it has inside, but those familiar with motor racing history might recognise the colour of the sign as "Bira blue", or know immediately that the white mouse is a nod to Thailand's first motor-racing heroes. Inside, the café contains precious memorabilia from the White Mouse team that competed in, and won, many Grand Prix and Formula One races around Europe in the 1930s.

The White Mouse story begins with two princes, the grandsons of Rama V, who lived in London. Prince Birabongse "Bira" Bhanudej was studying sculpture and his cousin Prince Chula Chakrabongse (seven years his senior) was writing biographies and establishing a literary career. Like their grandmother, Queen Saowaba (see p. 55 and p. 221), both princes had a passion for cars, and by 1935 Prince Bira was driving in short handicap races in a hyacinth-blue Riley Imp (the colour later became known as "Bira blue").

Bira, it turned out, was a natural talent behind the wheel. He moved on to driving an MG Magnette before his cousin bought him an English Racing Automobile for his 21st birthday. Prince Chula, known for his meticulous organisational skills, assembled a team of technicians and established White Mouse as a serious competitor in voiturette class motor racing.

The name "White Mouse" came from a Thai nickname for Prince Chula, and Prince Bira drew the cartoon mouse that was the team's emblem. "Bira blue", the favourite colour of Prince Chula's mother, became the team's official colour; it was combined with yellow, taken from Royal Standard of Thailand, and the two colours became the official racing colours of Thailand.

White Mouse Bar and Café today stands almost adjacent to Chakrabongse Villa, the family home of Prince Chula. Memorabilia in the café includes the steering wheel of Hanuman (one of the team's cars), as well as insignia, photographs, trophies, and books about racing, written by Prince Chula (some of which are for sale). There is also the official poster of the 1939 Bangkok Grand Prix, an event initiated by Prince Chula, but which never took place due to the outbreak of World War II.

MAI DUT AT CHAKRI MAHA PRASAT THRONE HALL

Outstanding examples of Thai topiary

Grand Palace
Na Phra Lan Road
Phra Nakhon
royalgrandpalace.th
Daily 8.30am–3.30pm
Dress code: conservative. It is best to wear long trousers or a skirt below the knee, shirts with a respectable neckline and sleeves that reach the elbow or below. Ripped jeans, shorts, short skirts and tight trousers, including leggings, may not be worn. Shoulders may not be exposed. See-through clothes may not be worn.

M̲ai dut is a form of topiary that has been practised in Thailand since the late Ayutthaya period, and some of the finest examples can be found within the walls of Bangkok's Grand Palace. The Chakri Maha Prasat Throne Hall, in particular, has magnificent (and old) *mai dut* trees that border the front lawn.

To the uninformed eye, these trees might look like haphazardly shaped but well-tended topiaries – however, they actually follow some of the nine traditional *mai dut* designs. The features of the designs include the shape of the main trunk, the number and angle of branches, and the number of "bouquets" of leaves on each branch. The *mai kabuan* form, for example, is a tree that grows straight and has a rising procession of five, seven or nine bouquets. *Mai chak* is considered the most challenging form of *mai dut*, where the branches grow in a series of 90-degree angles. Another traditional form is *mai ainchai*, where the tree trunk grows straight and then leans at an angle, like a tree growing off a cliff.

Mai dut is usually practised on fast-growing evergreen plants that have small, pointed leaves, including a relative of the ebony tree called *tako na* (*Diospyros rhodocalyx*), and *makham* or tamarind (*Tamarindus indica*). *Mai dut* was a pastime of court officials during the reign of Rama V (1868 to 1910) and since then it has been practised more widely, with modern practitioners leaning towards creating forms such as elephants and temple guardians instead of shapes. You will find more information on *mai dut* in the book *Sakul Intakul's Floral Journey Bangkok*, which is sold at the Museum of Floral Culture (see p. 238).

The controversial palace building

Rama V had wanted a Western-style home, and so the Chakri Maha Prasat Throne Hall, built in 1882, was designed by British architect John Clunich. Many people in the court were outraged that there was nothing "Siamese" about the design, and as a compromise the three domed roofs were replaced with Prasat spires.

Look carefully at the façade and you will see the emblem of the Chakri dynasty, which is two intertwined weapons: a three-bladed sword (*trisula*, the weapon of the god Shiva) and a throwing disc (*chakra*, the weapon of the god Vishnu).

WAT PHRA KAEW MUSEUM

A very good and little-known introduction to the Grand Palace complex

Grand Palace
Na Phra Lan Road, Phra Nakhon
royalgrandpalace.th
Daily 8.30am–3.30pm
Dress code: conservative. It is best to wear long trousers or a skirt below the knee, shirts or tops with a respectable neckline with sleeves that almost reach the elbow, or below. Ripped jeans, shorts, short skirts or tight trousers, including leggings, are not permitted. Shoulders must not be showing. See-through clothes must not be worn.

A s soon as they have bought their Grand Palace entrance tickets, most visitors rush to Wat Phra Kaew, the Temple of the Emerald Buddha. While this temple complex is absolutely astounding, there is a better "first stop": Wat Phra Kaew Museum. This quiet museum, which is tucked away near a rarely visited corner of the Grand Palace grounds, is not mentioned on the palace website or in its tourist information, yet it offers interesting insights into the history of the palace complex. Come here first, and your visit to the Grand Palace will take on so much more meaning.

The building that houses the museum was constructed during the reign of Rama V (1868 to 1910), and used to be the Royal Mint. In 1982, when Wat Phra Kaew underwent extensive renovations in preparation for Bangkok's bicentenary, it was decided that the Royal Mint become a museum.

The museum houses various artefacts from the palace complex: stone statues from the gardens; pieces of *chaw fa* (the ornate, sweeping "tips" that adorned roofs) and other architectural elements from Wat Phra Kaew. There are also Buddha images that were donated to the Emerald Buddha by various royalty. Also showcased are beautiful pieces of gold jewellery, utensils with intricate mother of pearl inlays, precious pieces of porcelain, royal couches (they are not as lavish as you would expect), the bones of white elephants (called *chang samkhan* in Thai, white elephants are symbols of royal power), and a collection of canons.

On the second floor of the museum a large model shows what the palace complex looked like in the 1780s. Buildings were added during the reign of various kings, and a second model depicts the property as it has stood since 1971.

How to find this "secret" museum

To locate the Wat Phra Kaew Museum, download the map from the Architecture page of the Grand Palace website – the museum is indicated on that map by the number 32. When you enter the Grand Palace, go to the museum first and buy the booklet *History of the Temple of the Emerald Buddha* by Professor MC Subhadradis Diskul (available in a variety of languages). Find a quiet spot within the palace complex to flip through this booklet before entering the Temple of the Emerald Buddha, because once you leave that temple you will not be allowed back in.

THE WOODEN PILLAR
OF THE CITY PILLAR SHRINE

㉕

The home of Bangkok's guardian spirit

2 Lak Muang Road, Phra Nakhon
Daily 6.30am–6.30pm

L ak Mueang, Bangkok's City Pillar Shrine, is a striking building. Its symmetry and layers give a very regal air to what many consider to be the most important structure in Bangkok: the shrine is home to Chao Pho Lak Mueang, the guardian spirit of the city.

It is not the shrine itself that provides the deity residence, but the wooden pillar inside. It was erected as the foundation stone of the new capital by Rama I, just after sunrise on 21 April 1782 – a particularly auspicious date, chosen by royal astrologers to ensure the prosperity of the new city. The pillar, now covered with gold lacquer, is surrounded by flowers and elephant tusks (in traditional Thai culture elephants are considered protectors) and is watched over by five guardian spirits.

People come here to make offerings, pay their respects and to ask favours of the deities. It is said that to ask for a favour, you should arrive at the shrine before 11am because at that time Chao Pho Lak Mueang ascends to heaven for the rest of the day. Even so, every day between 9am and 3.30pm dancing and music are performed at the shrine as entertainment for the other deities.

Erecting a city pillar was a custom of the Brahmins (see p. 42), and the origin of Bangkok's pillar can be traced back to the days when the region's kingdoms were at war. As with so many aspects of life here, astrology was carefully intertwined into preparations for attacks, and the commanders-in-chief of the armies would consult astrologers to determine auspicious days and times to carry out the attacks.

It was also important to ensure that the morale of the troops remained high – one of the astrological ceremonies performed for this reason was *tat mai khom nan* – to disgrace the enemy in effigy before a battle in order to encourage one's own troops. *Tat mai* means to cut wood, and so this part of the ceremony entailed felling a laburnum tree (*Cassia fistula*), which is called *chaiyapruek* in Thai, meaning "tree of success".

Before he ascended the throne as Rama I, General Chakri led the Thai army in a series of battles against the Burmese, and the tree that was felled before the final battle was 15 feet long – and it was this timber that in 1782 was laid as the foundation stone of Bangkok.

SILPA BHIRASRI MUSEUM

The studio of Thailand's "Father of Modern Art"

Silpakorn University – Fine Arts Department
Naphrathat Road, Phra Nakhon
Monday to Friday 9am–4pm

On the campus of Silpakorn University there is an intimate museum that celebrates the life and work of Italian sculptor Silpa Bhirasri (1892–1962), the man regarded as Thailand's Father of Modern Art. The two rooms, which were once the sculptor's office and studio, display memorabilia that include his books, tools, drawings, awards, notebooks and even cutlery. There are also framed personal letters written by Bhirasri that show genuine affection for his adopted country.

Until he was 54 years old, Bhirasri's name was Corrado Feroci – he changed it when he was granted Thai citizenship in 1946. Feroci was born in Tuscany and graduated from the Academy of Fine Arts in Florence, where he taught before Rama VI invited him to teach Western sculpture at Thailand's Fine Arts Department. It was in 1924 that Feroci moved to Bangkok, the city in which he then lived for the rest of his life.

In 1933, when European artists like Duchamp and Dali were painting dreams and exploring the unconscious mind with their Surrealist works, Feroci established Thailand's first school of modern art. It was granted university status in 1943, and its name evolved from the University of Fine Arts to Silpakorn University when its founder became a Thai citizen.

Many of the important sculptures in Bangkok were created by Bhirasri, including the King Rama I Monument near Memorial Bridge (see p. 186), the Democracy Monument on Ratchadamnoen Klang Road, the Victory Monument on Phahonyothin Road, the Rama VI Monument in Lumpini Park, and the King Taksin Monument in Thonburi. Plaster casts of many of Bhirasri's sculptures are kept in the Hall of Sculpture (see p. 68), adjacent to the museum.

Visit the home of Silpa Bhirasri

At 153 Ratchawithi Road (a 30-minute drive from the museum), Dusit, a mustard yellow neo-Renaissance house stands out in a neighbourhood of modern multi-storey buildings. "Silpa Bhirasri's Place", as the sign outside reads, was once the home of Silpa Bhirasri. These days the ground floor is a very pleasant coffee shop that displays an interesting collection of memorabilia: photos of the sculptor and his family, a bronze bust and information on some of his sculptures found around Bangkok. The second floor is used for art exhibitions.

HALL OF SCULPTURE

27

The hidden workshop where master sculptors worked

Silpakorn University – Fine Arts Department
Naphrathat Road, Phra Nakhon
Monday to Friday 9am–4pm

Tucked away on the campus of Silpakorn University, the Hall of Sculpture holds the works of some of Thailand's most revered sculptors. It is such a secret spot that even the campus guards might not know where it is.

From the early 1940s until the late 1980s the airy warehouse-like building was the foundry for the School of Fine Arts, and it was here that so many of Thailand's commemorative sculptures were created. In 1987 the foundry moved elsewhere, but plaster casts of some of the work created here – including sculptures of the Buddha, Thai royalty, heroes and heroines – are displayed in what is now called the Hall of Sculpture. Many of the works are by Silpa Bhirasri (see p. 66), as well as the renowned Thai sculptors Suporn Sirasongkroah, Pakorn Lekson and Sanan Silakorn.

It is quite a surreal feeling walking through the light-filled hall and seeing, close up, the plaster casts that were an intimate part of the sculpting process. There is only a small amount of information in English, but the hall is well worth a visit to see the early versions of some of Thailand's most revered sculptures.

The story of a Thai heroine

In the Hall of Sculpture one plaster cast is labelled "Thao Suranari (A Heroine from Thai History, Rattanakosin Period)" – a very simple description for the heroine with a fascinating story.

In 1825 Prince Anuwongse, ruler of Vientiane (which at that time was a vassal of Siam), travelled to Bangkok for the cremation of Rama II. His relationship with Siam was soon strained, however, as Rama III refused the prince's request for a troupe of ballerinas (the king did not like ballet): he also refused to return the descendants of Vientiane families who had been captured 50 years earlier.

In 1826 the prince planned a revolt. En route to Bangkok his army destroyed the town of Korat, 260 km north-east of Bangkok, and took thousands of men and women hostage, including Thao Suranari (1771–1852). The men were held in captivity, but the women were ordered to tend to the needs of the army – until one evening, under the leadership of Thao Suranari, the women lured the soldiers into a drunken orgy, and freed their captured men.

The image of Thao Suranari, sculpted in 1934 by Silpa Bhirasri, now stands in the city of Korat.

FIRST THAI TYPEWRITER

28

The reason two Thai characters were lost

Bangkok National Museum
Exhibition Hall 601 (Phra Wiman, the Viceroy Residential Complex)
Na Phra That Alley, Phra Nakhon
museumthailand.com
Wednesday to Sunday 8.30am–4pm

The heavy typewriter in exhibition hall 601 might not garner much attention, but it is worth a closer look. This old 78-key machine was the very first typewriter to contain Thai characters – and it is also the reason that two characters have fallen from use in the written Thai script.

This typewriter was not manufactured with the Thai character keys that you can see here: it was adapted in 1891 by Edwin Hunter McFarland, the son of an American missionary, who was born in Bangkok and served in the Ministry of Education. While on holiday in the USA, McFarland adapted this Smith Premier No 1 typewriter to display Thai characters.

McFarland ran into a problem, however – there were not enough keys to accommodate all the characters. By royal decree, he omitted *khor khoat* and *khor koh*, two of the lesser-used consonants, thus enabling the rest of the characters to fit onto the keyboard.

These two consonants have since fallen out of use in Thai script. Since typewriters were first used by the Royal Household, as writer Mohamed El-Fers explains in his book *Historic ABC of Thailand* (Vanity Press, 2012), it was considered a sign of loyalty to the king to drop the two consonants from handwritten Thai.

When McFarland died in 1896, the rights of his invention were passed on to his brother, the doctor/dentist George Bradley McFarland, and the first shipment of Thai typewriters was sent to Bangkok that same year.

The layout of Thai keyboards used today has evolved since 1896. The old Smith Premier No 1 typewriter, which was patented in 1890, did not have the benefit of a shift key, and so there were 78 keys to accommodate both upper-case and lower-case letters, as well as numbers and symbols. (It was also designed with an upstrike bar arrangement, meaning that the typists could not see what they were writing.) The modern Thai keyboard, configured in what is known as the Thai Kedmanee layout, has 59 keys.

The Thai alphabet

King Pho Khun Ramkhamaeng, who ruled over the Sukhothai Kingdom from 1279 to 1298, is credited with creating the Thai alphabet. There are 44 basic consonants (each with an inherent vowel), 18 other vowels, and six diphthongs (sounds created by the combination of two vowels) that are indicated with diacritics (symbols that are placed above, below or beside a letter).

RAMA IV'S GLOBE

A gift from Queen Victoria

Bangkok National Museum
Exhibition Hall 601 (Phra Wiman, the Viceroy Residential Complex)
Na Phra That Alley, Phra Nakhon
museumthailand.com
Wednesday to Sunday, 8.30am–4pm

In 1855 Queen Victoria sent an array of gifts to Rama IV. Many were damaged in transit, but two that arrived intact, namely a 36-inch globe and a miniature steam engine, are now on display at the Bangkok National Museum.

Queen Victoria sent these offerings as the ratification of the Treaty of Friendship and Commerce – the Bowring Treaty, as it is commonly known, liberalised trade restrictions and ultimately opened Thailand up to the West.

Rama IV had a particular interest in astronomy so one would assume the king would have been delighted to receive the globes (the queen sent him two, but only one is on display at the museum). As a monk, Rama IV had enjoyed discussing Earth's shape with intellectuals, according to Thai historian Thongchai Winichakul in his book *Siam Mapped: A History of the Geo-Body of a Nation* (University of Hawaii Press, 1997). Rama IV "was said to have abandoned the cosmology of the Traiphum [see below] before 1836. He had a globe, a chart calculating the coming eclipse, and maps in his room".

To the disbelief of Thai astrologers (who had considered a solar eclipse impossible), Rama IV predicted that there would be a total eclipse of the sun on 18 August 1868. It would be seen best near a remote village in southern Thailand, the king calculated, noting specifically where his pavilion should be positioned for the event. Part of the jungle was cleared, and a wooden palace, a pavilion and guesthouses were built for the Royal Court and a large party of international scientists, Thai astrologers and honoured guests.

The king's prediction proved accurate, but tragedy followed. While staying at that low-lying spot Rama IV contracted malaria, which led to his death two months after the eclipse.

The asteroid "151834 Mongkut", discovered in March 2003, was named after the king in recognition of his contribution to astronomy.

The cosmology of the Traiphum: a flat Earth

According to Theraveda Buddhist cosmology, the religious universe is comprised of the Traiphum, or three worlds: the sensual world, the form world and the formless world. Within these worlds there are 31 planes of existence, and through rebirth, we progress through these planes as we reach for Nirvana. According to the Traiphum, Earth is flat.

At the Museum Siam (see p. 56), there is a room containing blackboards showing intricate line drawings (and no explanation in English). These drawings are representations of the Traiphum.

TON-PHRO TREE

A sacred bodhi tree with a crowd of thirsty spirits

33 Soi Ram Butri, Phra Nakhon
Daily 8am–6pm (the gateway into the temple is locked overnight)

on-Phro Tree, one of Bangkok's majestic sacred bodhi trees, stands almost totally overlooked just a few metres away from the travellers who gather on Soi Ram Butri. It grows in the grounds of Wat Chana Songkhram and can be seen if you enter a partially hidden door in the temple wall (which, incidentally, is a convenient shortcut to the western end of the popular Khao San Road). There is a sign claiming the celebrated tree is 200 years old, but it is likely to be older: no-one knows when this tree first took root, and botanists now believe that *Ficus religiosa* (which is what Buddha sat under when he reached enlightenment) may live as long as 3,000 years.

Bodhi trees are instantly recognisable by their prominent heart-shaped leaves but in Bangkok (and in all of Thailand) they are even easier to spot: bodhi trees will almost always be wrapped in brightly coloured strands of fabric. Traditional belief in Thailand – an intricate weave of Buddhism, Hinduism and animism – is that these trees are home to *phi ton mai* (ghost that resides in a tree), and so to pay their respects to these spirits, people will tie strands of fabric around the tree's trunk and place offerings at the base. Different types of ghosts and spirits live in different species of trees (see p. 132 and p. 172). Some will have a specific purpose, but generally offerings are made to appease the spirits, and to give thanks if a wish has been granted.

"A bottle of strawberry Fanta can be worth 10 wishes to a benevolent spirit"

Next to the Ton-Phro Tree stands a typical Thai spirit house (see p. 80), and on its veranda you are sure to see several bottles of strawberry Fanta, all opened and with straws inserted conveniently in the bottlenecks. There are those who hypothesise that it is the blood-red colouring that made this drink a natural and very popular choice for offerings around Thailand. Whatever the case, it is interesting to note that despite the fact that few Thais would actually drink it, Thailand is the world's biggest consumer market for red Fanta.

The doorway through the back of Wat Chana Songkhram is locked at night, but if you come here first thing in the morning, you are likely to see the stall-holders from Ram Butri making their early offering at the Ton-Phro Tree in return for what they hope will be a fruitful day: "A bottle of strawberry Fanta can be worth 10 wishes to a benevolent spirit," they will tell you.

KHON COSTUME SEAMSTRESSES

The last seamstresses of a timeless tradition

Trok Khian Niwat and Trok Kai Chae, off Phra Sumen Road, Phra Nakhon
Daily 8am–5pm

Two quiet alleys off Phra Sumen Road are home to the few remaining seamstresses whose work is essential to the greatest of Thailand's performing arts: the embroidery of elaborate Khon costumes. Khon is a traditional narrative dance that, through a fusion of literature, fine art, music, craft and dance, is a remarkable performance of the Ramakian epic. It dates back to the Ayutthaya era when it was performed by men in the royal court. The artform has now been inscribed by Unesco on the Intangible Heritage List for its unique musical, vocal, dance, ritual and handicraft elements.

Central to the Khon spectacle are the masks and incredibly intricate costumes that indicate the characters, which range from gods to demons. These are carefully created by weavers, mask-makers, jewellers, tailors and the seamstresses who hand-embroider the costumes.

"I've been working on this same small stretch of bordering for five days," explains Wanna Nimprasert as she looks up from hand-stitching fine silver thread onto white cotton. The work is so painstaking that Mrs Nimprasert might only stitch a few inches of bordering each day, yet her fingers end up sore and swollen, and apart from a whirring electric fan, there is little about her workstation that would not have been familiar to a royal seamstress from two centuries ago.

As many as 100 dancers are involved in a Khon performance – the costumes (which cost around US$650 each) have no buttons or zippers and must be stitched onto the dancers. Strict colour codes are used for the characters, Mrs Nimprasert explains, but the stylised patterns embroidered often vary from seamstress to seamstress. Cotton, satin and metallic threads are favoured, and candle wax is often used to lubricate the thread.

Somkid Laothong, a seamstress in neighbouring Trok Kai Chae alley, is famous for rarely taking a day off. She is immortalised in a photograph displayed in the nearby Pipit Banglamphu Museum (see p. 78). "The intricate work reflects the utmost skills and pride of the artist who spends countless hours crafting such a sophisticated look," the caption points out.

Khon performances have been given at Sala Chalermkrung Royal Theatre (66 Chalermkrung Road, Phra Nakhon) since the 1930s. There is a beautiful Khon costume display at the Rattanakosin Exhibition Hall (see p. 24).

PIPIT BANGLAMPHU MUSEUM

A window into old-time Banglamphu

Phra Sumen Rd, Phra Nakhon,
Tuesday to Sunday 10am–6pm

You are unlikely to describe the sleepy backstreets of Banglamphu quarter as an "industrial area", but if there is one industry that is still thriving here, it is printing. The main reason for this is that the big white building next to Phra Sumen Fort was originally Thailand's first printing school, but that building and the adjacent 150-year-old stilted timber structure are now occupied by Pipit Banglamphu Museum.

The impressive interactive museum offers colourful and fun insights into Banglamphu's local heritage. Several rooms are dedicated to the National Treasury and Thailand's beloved Queen Sirikit (Queen Mother of Thailand), but the most enticing aspect is the vast upper-storey maze that takes you on a rambling interactive wander through the many icons of Banglamphu.

The journey takes you back to a time even before the canal was built (see p. 22): a secret lever hidden in a bookshelf opens a door, and you will find yourself sitting in a mock rowing boat in what appears to be a dark night, lit only by fireflies that flit between the *lamphu* trees (*Duabanga grandiflora*), after which the quarter was named, and the last of which can be found in the little park surrounding Phra Sumen Fort. Farther on there is a mock-up of a Thai cinema and a tram-stop (neither of which exist these days in Banglamphu). There are evocative alcoves that bring to life vintage coffee shops, gramophone shops and cobblers, and there are fascinating displays explaining some of the disappearing (or disappeared) crafts and arts for which the quarter was once famous, such as ceremonial banana trunk carving and traditional embroidery (see p. 76).

These exhibits, titled *Si San Banglamphu* (The Colours of Banglamphu) and *Tin Khon Dee Sri Banglamphu* (Good People of Banglamphu), are not only great fun but are the perfect preparation for wandering further north of the canal into one of Bangkok's most atmospheric quarters.

SPIRIT HOUSE ON PHRA SUMEN ROAD

A home for the spirits in an historic palace gateway

52/1 Phra Sumen Road, Phra Nakhon

T he neat row of little eateries and barbers opposite Pipit Banglamphu Museum (see p. 78) is interrupted by a crumbling red brick wall. However, you would be unlikely to notice it if it were not for the spirit house that stands there, and which is always shrouded with elaborate *phuang malai* (flower garlands). The two sections of wall create what was once a gateway and are now the final remnants of the palace of one of Rama I's sons. The small sections of wall on either side of the spirit house are now preserved (barely), and revered by the inhabitants of this quarter as a relic of times past.

You will notice that even among the clustered buildings on Phra Sumen Road, no developer has imposed building plans upon the spirit house which guards the remnants of the palace. This is fortunate not only for the walls, but also for the stray cats in the quarter since a donation box stands there, allowing people to make merit (see p. 19) by donating money for cat food.

Spirit houses

Spirit houses (*phra phum chaothi*) are erected to appease the spirits of historical sites and sacred trees (see p. 74), and they are built to placate the resident spirits when new structures are erected. Thai people tend to maintain a very practical blend of Buddhist, Hindu and animist (spirit and ancestor worship) beliefs, and it would be considered foolhardy for anyone to construct a building – whether a simple home or a multi-storey mall – without ensuring that the resident *Phra Phum* (Lord of the Land) has his own dwelling. The spirit house almost always stands on pillars and has an inner room as well as a platform, where daily offerings of food, drinks, incense and *phuang malai* are placed.

Before a building is designed, the most propitious location for the spirit house is established, and common belief is that the spirit house and the "real" house should never throw a shadow over each other. The building and maintenance of a spirit house is considered the primary form of housing insurance, and stories abound of the terrible things that happened when the tradition was ignored and the "evicted" spirits became vindictive (see p. 92). Likewise, removing or relocating a spirit house involves an expensive and complex ritual which, because of the risk involved, is often even grander than the ceremony that took place when the house was erected.

SAI BAHT ON SOI KRAISI

Giving alms to monks at dawn

Soi Kraisi, Phra Nakhon
Daily, first light until about 8am

Y ou might be surprised to come across one of Bangkok's most spiritual wake-up calls just a few blocks from the backpacker ghetto of Khao San Road, but Soi Kraisi is an ideal place to witness *sai*

baht, people giving alms to monks on their evocative barefoot dawn pilgrimages, or *bin ta baht*. Soi Kraisi is a residential neighbourhood, and many people habitually leave home before dawn to visit market stalls – not only for the freshest vegetables, but also to make offerings.

According to Buddhist tradition, the monks should receive their food before the local populace can eat. As a long procession of monks from a nearby monastery turns into the street, the stall-holders, shoppers and commuters begin to stand in line to offer them sustenance. Residents line up too, waiting for an opportunity to offer alms in return for karmic blessings. They do not expect the monks to acknowledge their offering

in any way, or even to make eye-contact. The monk should keep his eyes focussed only on the bowl – for him to express thanks would be considered highly inappropriate since it is he who is effectively offering the populace an opportunity to make merit (see p. 19).

Bangkokians are fanatical about food and even at this early hour the street is lined with stands selling everything from pungent dried squid to spicy *pad thai*. Grab a table at one of the pavement stalls and order a plate of delicious *kanom krok* (bite-sized coconut puddings) and a glass of chilled *bolan* coffee. *Bolan* simply means "old style" and this coffee is always served the traditional way: cold, strong and poured through a cloth filter that looks disturbingly like an old sock. Time your arrival at Soi Kraisi for around first light – an early breakfast at one of the street-side stalls in this peaceful and atmospheric setting might just prove to be one of the most enduring memories of your time in the City of Angels.

Bowling alleys of a different kind

In a tangle of alleys off Soi Ban Bat near the Golden Mount, there is a little community that is among the last to produce hand-made *baht* (alms bowls). There are 300,000 monks in Thailand, and virtually all of them use *baht* bowls. These days most are factory-made, but the Ban Bat community continues to hammer their produce out by hand, as they always did, from slabs of steel.

SCORPIONS ON SOI RAM BUTRI

Bangkok's culinary initiation rite

Soi Ram Butri, Chakkra Phong Road, Phra Nakorn
Daily 6pm–12 midnight

A s it is just a two-minute walk from the popular backpacker hangout of Khao San Road, few would claim that Soi Ram Butri is a secret spot. Nevertheless, this street remains overlooked by the majority of visitors who make a beeline for Khao San's nightlife. This is a shame because Soi Ram Butri is home to a few surprises for the first-time visitor to Bangkok, and scorpion and tarantula lollipops are likely to be top of the list.

Grasshoppers, crickets, bamboo grubs, giant water beetles and any of Thailand's three tarantula species are among a vast array of insects that are commonly eaten in rural Thailand. Visitors are often stunned to see all of these on sale along Soi Ram Butri. Few people realise that the nocturnal insect sellers make the majority of their revenue not from actual diners, but from charging "modelling fees". There is a price levied on *farang* (foreigners) who want to get a snapshot or a selfie but would never intend to actually sample these delicacies.

It is interesting that these culinary morsels have become an attraction for tourists alone, in this area at least. Business has boomed so spectacularly that scorpion farms have been established in rural Thailand in an effort to keep up with demand: it is probable that the insects are actually becoming less common (and less affordable) as a snack for people living in those rural areas.

The stingers and venom glands are normally removed before eating, but do not worry if you forget, because as long as they are well cooked, the venom breaks down during cooking. Claims that the scorpions are an aphrodisiac are untrue, but when fried in oil, they are crunchy, tasty and high in protein. Some experts claim that while beef contains about 20 percent protein content, scorpions are packed with as much as 80 percent.

"Many Thais love fried bugs," stall holder Bi Toci explains. "We used to eat them often at my village near Chiang Mai but these days I only sell to *farang*." Bi Toci's prices have been inflated by her tourist clientele to the point where few Thais would spend as much as US$3 on a single scorpion or tarantula. Yet every backpacker with an ounce of gumption feels that it is a sort of right-of-passage to sample Bangkok's famous insect street-food at least once.

Chinatown

CHAO KROM POE PHARMACY

Bangkok's oldest pharmacy

229–231 Chakkrawat Road, Samphanthawong
Monday to Saturday 8am–4.30pm

On Chakkrawat Road you will be struck by the aroma of mysterious roots and spices long before you reach Chao Krom Poe, a pharmacy founded by Peasuwan Temy in 1896. His descendants have been running the business in the same premises ever since.

Chao Krom Poe Pharmacy stocks over 750 traditional Thai medicinal products, from roots, flowers and leaves to dried animal parts and crushed minerals. There is a consulting desk where customers are treated with remedies (cure-alls, potions, poultices, infusions and balms) created from a recipe book started by the founder himself. The medicine dispensed here can be astonishingly potent: the pharmacy's website advises that clay, enamel, steel or glass pots should be used to boil the herbs, and that aluminium pots should never be used because "some drugs will eat away the aluminium".

In Grandmother's House (Monsoon Books, 2011), a fascinating book about Thai folklore and traditions, some surprising traditional Thai remedies are listed: safflower stalks for toothache, sawtooth coriander as an ointment for venomous insect bites, drops of garlic juice to cure ear infection, charred kaffir limes for shampoo, and turmeric as an antiseptic for cuts or to cure acne, and sometimes as an antidote to cobra venom.

Traditional Thai medicine has its roots in the animist traditions of the Mon and Khmer people. In the early 1900s it was shunned in favour of modern medicine, but in the mid-1990s there was move to revive traditional medicine.

Those who have a particular interest in medicine might like to see the collection of raw materials used in traditional medicine at the Museum of Natural Medicines at Chulalongkorn University (3rd floor Osothsala Building, Phyathai Road, Pathum Wan. Open Wednesdays and Thursdays 9am–12pm).

NEARBY
Baan Mowaan
9 Soi Thesa Bamroongmuang Road, Phra Nakon
Daily 9am–5pm
mowaan.com

Baan Mowaan is a fascinating pharmacy and museum. This beautiful Sino-Portuguese townhouse, winner of an Architectural Conservation Award, has been so lovingly preserved that it appears much as it did when Dr Waan Rod-Muang first opened his shop here in 1924. The traditional doctor's great-grandchildren continue to dispense the same medicines that the shop's founder did for members of the Thai royal family almost a century ago.

WAT KHANIKAPHON

A temple paid for by prostitutes

416 Phlap Phla Chai Road, Pom Prap Sattru Phai
Daily 6am–6pm

"Temple Built With Earnings From Prostitution" seems an unlikely name for a religious place, but on a busy corner in Chinatown, there it stands: Wat Khanikaphon, a small temple whose name acknowledges the profession of the women who paid for it.

The temple was built in 1833 by Khun Yai Faeng, a devout Buddhist who owned a popular brothel in the historic Sampheng neighbourhood. Along with the women who worked for her, Grandmother Faeng, as she was affectionately known, saved money to build the temple. After it was completed the temple remained nameless – something quite common in those days – and people referred to it simply as Wat Mai Yai Faeng (Grandmother Faeng's New Temple).

Decades after it was built renovations were carried out. By this time Grandmother Faeng had passed away and her descendants asked Rama V to name the temple. Wat Khanikaphon was the name he bestowed upon it, meaning "Temple Built With Earnings From Prostitution".

People still pay their respects to Grandmother Faeng. There is a gold-coloured bust of the old woman in a small shrine behind the temple, where her shoulders are draped in lace and strings of plastic pearls have been placed around her neck. There is another statue of Grandmother Faeng in the *viharn* (sermon hall). She sits at the back, facing a collection of Buddha images, and is surrounded by offerings of flowers, draped with pink "pearl" necklaces and encircled by an assortment of make-up.

The green lanterns of Bangkok: how prostitutes showed that their taxes were paid

When Grandmother Faeng ran her brothel more than 200 years ago, prostitution was legal in Siam and there were about 40 registered "prostitute houses" in the Sampheng area. The earliest records of the profession in Thailand date back to 1680, when an official in Ayutthaya received a licence to run an elite brothel – it is reported that 600 women, including the daughters of esteemed officers, worked there. By the time of the reign of Rama V (1868 to 1910), prostitutes were subject to taxation and regular health checks. To show that their taxes were paid, prostitutes would hang a green lantern outside their premises, and some say that the green tiles around the windows at Wat Khanikaphon are a nod to Grandmother Faeng's green lantern. Prostitution was declared illegal in Thailand in 1960.

ER GER FONG SHRINE

The shrine where gamblers ask for luck

447 Phlap Phla Chai Road, Pom Prap Sattru Phai
Daily 8am–6pm

Apart from buying lottery tickets and betting on horses, gambling is illegal in Thailand – yet in an ironic twist, people seeking good luck in their gambling endeavours climb four floors above a police station to pay their respects to "the gambling god". The rooftop shrine is dedicated not to a god, however, but to Por Phu Er Ger Fong (1851–1936), an exceptionally wealthy Chinese-Thai man who ran many of the gambling dens that were so prominent in Bangkok around the turn of the last century.

The story goes that before the police station was built, the original shrine for Por Phu Er Ger Fong stood on that land, and was demolished to make way for the new building. Once it was complete, a few policemen died in a run of accidents and it was agreed that the shrine should be rebuilt. The rooftop of the police station was the logical location.

The new shrine was established with clear reverence for the man it honours. In traditional Thai culture elephants are considered protectors and to bring good fortune, and at the shrine a regal statue of Por Phu Er Ger Fong is framed by two pairs of elephant tusks, as well as offerings of yellow flowers, cigars, black coffee, betel nut, Chinese tea and incense. "People come here to ask for good fortune," says Tanawat Jaogonun, who established the new shrine. "It depends on their merit. If they have good luck, Por Phu Er Ger Fong will help them quicker but if not then they must wait for their chance. It's not like everyone would get what they want; then there would be no poor and only the rich."

It is a well-known rule that anyone who finds fortune after visiting this shrine needs to share some of their winnings with those less fortunate, and they should return to the shrine pay their respects.

Por Phu Er Ger Fong was held in high regard during his lifetime and is now revered as a sacred figure. Today amulets containing his image are popular. The powerful businessman – who was also known by the names Phra Anuwat Rachaniyom, Tae Ti Yong and Yi Go Hong – went to great lengths to help the needy, and was a founder of Pô Tek Tueng, a charitable foundation established to help sick and wounded people and to take care of unidentified corpses. (In Thailand it is not uncommon for people to buy coffins for those who cannot afford them – see p. 154.)

CHAROEN CHAI NEIGHBOURHOOD

The community that sells flammable gifts for ghosts

Soi Charoen Chai, Charoen Krung Road, Pom Prap Sattru Phai

Situated between four of Bangkok's important Chinese temples, Charoen Chai is an intriguing neighbourhood where tradition and modern life blend seamlessly. It is here that joss paper – paper burnt as an offering to ancestors – is sold, just as it has been since the community first settled into the area's shophouses in the 1880s. The modern twist, however, is that most of the paper goods are not what you would have found 140, or even 40, years ago.

Charoen Chai is the last community selling joss paper in Bangkok. Here, amidst the red paper lanterns and sacred garlands of carefully folded red and gold paper, you will find pile upon pile of paper iPhones, laptops, Nikes, Rolexes, passports, US dollars (which you can only buy if you buy a "passport"), iPads, Louis Vuitton shoes ... even three-dimensional Mercedes Benz cars. The reason? Thai Chinese burn these paper goods during ceremonies and on auspicious occasions as an offering to their ancestors, so that the deceased may be comfortable in the afterlife.

The variety of joss paper on sale in Charoen Chai makes for an intriguing visit to this neighbourhood. Here you can catch a glimpse of traditional community life as you wander past old shophouses where tables weighed down by paper offerings jut out into the lanes.

A threat to the air quality of Bangkok

The paper goods add such rich colour to these tarpaulin-shaded alleys, but they add something more sinister too, namely a very real threat to the quality of air in Bangkok.

It might not seem too serious when one person burns a paper iPhone or Rolex, but when you consider that there could be more than 9 million people of Chinese descent living in Thailand, all that paper burning adds up. There is so much joss paper burnt on significant days such as Chinese New Year and Qingming Festival (also known as Tomb-Sweeping Day), that the smoke from these offerings has become a major contributor to air pollution in the city. While it is unlikely that this tradition will come to an end, many Thai Chinese families have decided to cut back on the amount of paper they burn at ceremonies. This may be good news for the environment, but reduced business could have dire consequences for a community that is already worried about its longevity in a city where space for new developments is at a premium.

HISTORIC HUT CHAROEN CHAI ⑤

The evocative old home of fortune tellers

*32 Soi Charoen Krung 23, Phlap Phla Chai Road, Pom Prap Sattru Phai
Daily 7am–6.30pm*

As you wander the *sois* (alleys) of Chinatown you will catch glimpses of life as it is lived on the street, but the spaces behind the alley-front stalls – the homes of the people who live and work here – remain private. In historic Charoen Chai neighbourhood, there is one little house where visitors are welcome, and it is an absolute delight to explore. Historic Hut Charoen Chai (also called Baan Kao Lao Rueng) is a community centre and museum, and it was established by the community to preserve their heritage.

This house, with its weathered turquoise doors, was once the home of Hia Hok Sae Pung and his father Pung Teng Lung Zean, both fortune tellers who were well known in Bangkok's Thai Chinese community. Pung Teng Lung Zean had moved to the city from China with his collection of astrological textbooks. Word of his talents spread, and people came from all over the city for advice on how best to negotiate life.

Relics of the fortune tellers' trade are displayed around the room upstairs, including old astrology books and the beautiful hand-painted wooden signs that once hung outside this house. The signs show different hands and faces, which are what the fortune tellers read to delve into a person's future: for example, the shape of one's nose gives details of one's wealth, the mouth discloses talent, eyebrows give an indication of health and longevity, and the forehead imparts details of one's luck. It is more complex than this, of course, and the fortune tellers would also take into account the proportions of the face, lines, wrinkles, and various points and markings.

It is fitting that the blue paper on the walls of this house is peeling away, revealing the layers beneath. On these walls hang black and white photographs that document the lives of the people who have lived in this neighbourhood for decades. Along with the fortune tellers' memorabilia, the tiny museum houses a collection of garments from the Chinese opera performers who also once lived in this house, as well as a few household knick-knacks and a collection of paper offerings that would certainly have come from the neighbourhood's joss paper shops (see p. 94).

LENG BUAI IA SHRINE

A visually intricate piece of history

34 Plaeng Nam Road, Samphanthawong
Daily 7am–5pm

Leng Buai Ia shrine is a small sanctuary in Sampheng neighbourhood – it is a visually intricate piece of history in an area cluttered with street stalls and shophouses. The pretty mosaics and bas-relief paintings of dragons and tigers, deities, flowers and lions – each one very carefully created and conveying a meaning – will appeal to any traveller who takes delight in studying details.

At the back of the shrine there are three figures – the middle image is that of a religious scholar named Koe Yi, who lived during the 14th century. His grave, in a Teochew-speaking district in China, became a popular pilgrimage destination, and when residents of that area moved elsewhere, they would often erect shrines in his honour in their new neighbourhood. The year that this shrine was built is not known, but what is certain is that it was in existence in 1782 when the Teochew-speaking Chinese community relocated to Sampheng from Rattanakosin, when the Grand Palace was built (see p. 20).

Most shrines in Sampheng are named after the presiding deity, but not this one. The name Leng Buai Ia means "shrine at the dragon's tail", and is a reference to the feng shui principle that in order for a building to be in harmony with the forces of nature, it should face a body of water and have its back to the mountains. In other words, the building faces the direction in which a dragon would travel to reach water from its lair. In the late 1700s, when the Sampheng district was new, this shrine was situated at what was considered the back of the dragon's tail (hence the name), but this is no longer the case. As Bangkok developed and more canals were built, the feng shui "flow" of Sampheng changed from running north-south to west-east. The direction of the dragon therefore shifted by 90 degrees, but the name of the shrine remained.

Leng Buai Ia is often said to be the oldest Chinese shrine in Thailand, but this is questionable. A plaque in the shrine has the date 1658, and it is on this that the "oldest temple" claim is based. However, Edward Van Roy in his enlightening book *Sampheng – Bangkok's Chinatown Inside Out* (Institute of Asian Studies, 2007), argues that the plaque could simply have been brought to this shrine from elsewhere, possibly a shrine in Ayutthaya that was destroyed during the Burmese siege in 1767.

FACE THREADERS
OF CHINATOWN

An age-old beauty treatment on the streets of Chinatown

Along much of the Chinatown section of Charoeng Krung Road,
Samphanthawong
Daily 9am–6pm

The ancient art of threading (known as *mang-ming* in Thai) is a traditional beauty treatment that has survived unchanged along the pavements of Charoeng Krung Road. Here, throughout the day, Bangkokians who want their facial hair neatened or removed sit on high stools amid a jostle of pedestrians while expert "threaders" skilfully take care of the unwanted fluff.

Cha-on Udomphonphoemthawi learned the threading technique from her mother and has been working on the pavement (near 600 Charoeng Krung Road) for more than two decades. To remove hair, a length of cotton is twisted and held between fingers and teeth, and the therapist then manipulates the cotton over the client's "problem" areas. Cha-on claims it is by far the best way to trim the contours of the eyebrows and to remove even the finest "peach-fuzz" on the cheekbones, and that it is far more effective (and less painful) than waxing or using tweezers. Powder – often a scented mixture of calcium carbonate and lime powder – is used to make the process smoother and stop the thread from burning the skin. Some customers believe that this also helps to whiten the skin.

A skilled threader is able to complete a full facial in about 20 minutes (at a price of around 100 baht). Although it is only slightly painful for the customers, a day's work can be tiring for the workers – Cha-on and her colleagues frequently end the day with very sore fingers and necks that are tense from pulling with their teeth.

In Thailand you are unlikely to see street-side threaders beyond the limits of Chinatown, but it is not a treatment that is confined to the Chinese world. Some experts claim that threading may have originated in India as long as 6,000 years ago, and there are historical records showing that it was traditionally a part of the wedding ritual for brides in both China and ancient Persia. Face threading formed part of the Intangible Cultural Heritage list for Hong Kong in 2014, where the treatment is fast disappearing from the streets (although it is more common in salons).

TANG TOH KANG GOLD SHOP AND MUSEUM

Bangkok's oldest gold shop

345 Wanit Road Soi 1, Samphanthawong
Monday to Saturday 9.30am–4pm

L ift your gaze above the frenzy of umbrellas, food vendors and street-side market stalls on the intersection of Wanit and Mangkon roads, and you will see a rather grand seven-storey European-style building rising above a mesh of powerlines. That building is the property of Tang Toh Kang, the oldest goldsmith business in an area considered to have one of the highest concentrations of gold shops in the world.

The shop is named after its founder, Mr Tang Toh, who built a reputation for honesty and fine craftsmanship. When he passed away the business was taken over by his son, Tang Tek-Kwang, who in 1921 was appointed by Rama VI as goldsmith to the royal household. There is now a private museum on the sixth floor, which houses a collection of tools and equipment from the shop's 140-year history. There are moulds and storage jars, goldsmiths' desks, tools, scales, abacus, an intriguing collection of stamps, the shop's old signs, and the two Garuda emblems given to the store by Rama VI, who adopted the Garuda as a national emblem for Thailand in 1911. Take time as you climb the stairs to the museum to appreciate the astounding collection of playing cards which are framed and on display on the staircase walls.

To understand the significance of this place and the impact it had on shaping the lives of those who lived here, one needs to be aware of what was happening in Bangkok in the 1880s, when Mr Tang Toh first opened his shop. The population of Chinese immigrants was growing fairly rapidly, drawn to Bangkok by the opportunities for work. Accumulating wealth plays a significant role in Chinese culture, but because many of the immigrants were considered "alien", they were not able to invest in property in Bangkok. As a means of investing their hard-earned cash, the Chinese immigrants took to buying gold ornaments and jewellery, and so the gold trade in the Yeowarat area began to flourish. It is estimated that these days there are almost 150 gold shops in the Yeowarat area.

Worth its weight ...
The standard weight unit for measuring gold in Thailand is the *baht* – and it was from this that the name for Thailand's currency was taken.

ROYAL EXECUTION STONE

Where traitorous royals met their fate

Wat Pathum Khongkha, 1620 Song Wat Road, Samphanthawong
Daily 5am–9pm

Wat Pathum Khongkha has long been associated with death, but beneath a bodhi tree in what is now a car park, a small pavilion makes the association even more sinister – the object of veneration is the stone slab on which royal executions were carried out.

The death penalty still exists in Thailand, and until 1932, the execution method was usually beheading. Members of the royal family, however, met their fate in a different manner. Royal blood was not allowed to be spilled, and so after being stripped of their royal titles, transgressors were beaten on the back of the neck with a sandalwood club. Some sources say a velvet bag would be placed over the head of the offending royal before they were laid on the stone, while others claim it was the corpses that were placed in a velvet bag.

The small pavilion in the grounds of Wat Pathum Khongkha was erected by the descendants of Prince Rakronaret who, in 1848, was the last royal to have been executed here. The prince, a son of Rama I and an uncle of Rama III (who was ruling at the time of the execution), was accused of abusing his power and privileges. Rama III set up a court of enquiry and the prince was found to have been accepting bribes, and plotting to become the next king.

Other royals executed on this stone at Wat Pathum Khongkha were also accused of high treason. In 1804 Prince Lamuan and Prince Inthapat, the sons of Rama I's *uparaja* (viceroy) were executed for plotting to overthrow Rama I. Five years later, just three days after Rama II ascended the throne, a senior minister received an anonymous letter stating that Celestial Prince Kasatra (a son of King Taksin, see p. 16) was among a group of officials planning a revolt. After an inquiry was launched the prince, along with 10 officials, admitted their plans and all were executed.

The submersion site for royal ashes

Wat Pathum Khongkha stands on the banks of the Chao Phraya River and for a few generations it was the submersion site for royal ashes. The Thai royal tradition was that after cremation the royal remains – usually shards of bone – would be placed in urns and enshrined in the Grand Palace. The ashes were then placed in a ceramic bowl, wrapped in white fabric, and carried upriver by royal barge to Wat Pathum Khongkha, where the bowl was lowered into the river.

Trace the roots of Chinatown

1 Soi 1620/1 Song Wat Road, Samphanthawong
Monday to Friday 9am–4pm

คนเก็บขายขวด ๒๕๓๖ สีน้ำ ๒๘.๓ x ๓๘ ซม.
A peddling recycler, 1993. Watercolour. 28.3 x 38 cm.
โดย จักรพันธุ์ โปษยกฤต

Chinatown is an intriguing combination of slick pockets of modern development and captivating corners of history. While simply wandering the streets is an exciting way to experience the district, a visit to the small Samphanthawong Museum will certainly provide a deeper appreciation and understanding of the area. It focuses on the lives of Bangkok's early Chinese immigrants, and their contribution to establishing Bangkok's economy.

The comprehensive information boards (written in Thai, Chinese and English) also give interesting insights into details, easily missed, of the surrounding area such as how some of the alleys got their names, intricate design features of some of the old shophouses, and where to find an unusual mosque. In the museum look for the large red poster of a street map – it is superimposed on the drawing of a dragon and shows how Yaowarat Road and its alleys represent the curving body of a dragon, making it an auspicious area for business. Taksin the Great (see p. 16), who liberated Siam after Ayutthaya fell to the Burmese, was of Chinese descent and the role he played in founding Bangkok is outlined here.

The Samphanthawong Museum is located in the administration building of the school that is directly over the road from Wat Phatum Khongka (see p. 110).

Chinese immigrant "status updates"

In the early Rattanakosin Era there was a shortage of Thai labour and so Chinese workers were welcomed into the city (see p. 162). They were mostly involved in construction, digging canals and working in the junk (boat) trade, which was the major source of income for Siam at that time.

The Chinese immigrants were marked in one of two ways to show that they were legitimately allowed to live in the country. Those who worked for an official had a mark tattooed onto their wrist, and the design of the tattoo indicated to which official they "belonged". Those who chose to pay *phuk pi*, a form of government tax that essentially bought their freedom, had a string tied around their wrist, with a wax seal placed over the knot. The string was replaced every six months (which was how often the taxes were paid) and the seal was pressed into a round shape with an official marking on it – similar to a *pi kra bueng*, or gambling token (see p. 226).

MUMMIFIED MONK

The monk who achieved nirvana

Patriarch's Hall
Wat U Phai Rat Bamrung, Charoen Krung Road, Samphanthawong
Daily 8am–6pm
Visitors are welcome to look inside the Patriarch's Hall, but it is usually locked.
Ask one of the monks to show you to the hall.

W at U Phai Rat Bamrung, an elaborately decorated temple built by Vietnamese immigrants in the late 1700s, has in one of its halls the naturally mummified body of the monk who was the fourth abbot of this temple.

Just before the body of Phra Kru Kana Num Samajarn (1900–1958) was to be cremated, the head of the Annam Nikai (the Vietnamese sect of Mahayana Buddhist temples) asked for the coffin to be opened, and saw that the body had dried, not decayed. The monk's body was moved to the Patriarch's Hall, where it still sits today in a glass case.

"We say he is *arahant*, the Pali word [see p. 236] we use for someone who has achieved nirvana," explained one of the monks who lives at the temple.

The Patriarch's Hall is adorned with photographs and biographies (in English, Vietnamese and Thai) of monks who have held esteemed positions here. There is also a collection of Buddha images, including one gifted by temple patron Rama V.

Rama IV was also a patron of this temple, and to show harmony between the two main branches of Buddhism – Mahayana and Theravada (the latter being the main religion in Thailand, practised by almost 95 percent of the population) – he invited Annam Nikai monks to participate in royal ceremonies. In 1861 they performed a ritual reserved for a departed saint at the funeral of Queen Debsirindra, Rama IV's queen consort, and four years later the monks performed a prayer service at the funeral of Rama IV's brother, Phra Pinklao (see p. 125). This ceremony, called Kong Tek, has been performed at all royal funerals ever since.

The sisters who became queens of Siam

Queen Debsirindra (1834–1861) was born Princess Ramphoei, the daughter of acclaimed artist Prince Siriwongse (also called Prince Mataya – look for the doors he inlaid with mother of pearl at the Bangkok National Museum). When he died aged 27, the princess and her sister, Princess Banarai, went to live with their grandfather, Rama III. Both sisters later married their great-uncle, Rama IV (see p. 55) and Queen Debsirindra, the queen consort, gave birth to Prince Chulalongkorn, who became Rama V. Princess Banarai was elevated to queen consort after her sister's death (but she was not given the title of queen). She is said to be the inspiration for the character Lady Thiang in Anna Leonowens's well-known book *The King and I* (see p. 74).

SOL HENG TAI MANSION

(12)

An unexpected architectural jewel in a hidden alley

282 Soi Wanit 2, Samphanthawong
Tuesday to Sunday 9am–6pm

In the midst of the oil-puddled streets of Chinatown's "Tin Pan Alley", there is an ornate scarlet doorway that leads into one of Bangkok's most unexpected and enchanting courtyards. The fact that its patio was converted into a swimming pool in 2004 – creating what must surely be one of the world's most bizarrely located dive schools – does surprisingly little to detract from the property's timeless beauty.

Phra Aphaivanich (sometimes written Aphaiwanit) was a collector of taxes levied on edible birds' nests, and built Sol Heng Tai Mansion about 200 years ago. It soon became the control centre and think tank for virtually everything that happened in Talat Noi quarter. He owned many buildings in the neighbourhood and the mansion housed the headquarters of his powerful business empire.

The Posayajinda and Chatikavanij families who live here today are the eighth-generation descendants of the original Sol clan who owned most of the quarter.

The outer doors of Sol Heng Tai are decorated with propitious phrases written in Cantonese, and the teak buildings inside follow the *si tiam kim* (golden four points) style of architecture – four buildings surrounding a

courtyard. The property has been recognised as an architectural gem and in 1982, as part of Bangkok's bicentenary celebrations, it underwent a thorough 10 million-baht renovation. Lately funds have been in short supply, and the owners have struggled to maintain the property, with business plans ranging from the dive school to a breeding kennel for beagles and now, a small café.

When you visit what is still a family home, look out for the iron safe where the family gold was once stored. "They kept gold bars in

iron trunks that were so heavy they made the floor sink," the owners say. "The ceiling was strung with bells which would ring as a warning if anybody walked on the roof."

Despite these measures, it is said that more than 40 chests full of gold were stolen over the years by a string of very innovative thieves – the most original of whom applied vinegar over the course of many days to dissolve the lime in the crushed seashell and sugarcane walls so that he could silently enter the family vault from an adjacent building.

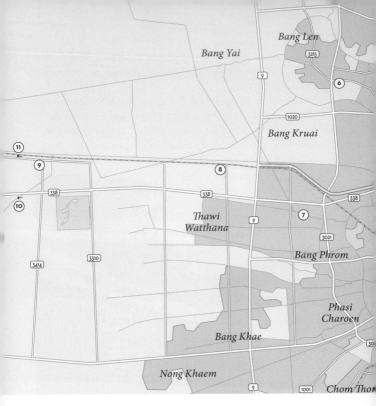

Bangkok West

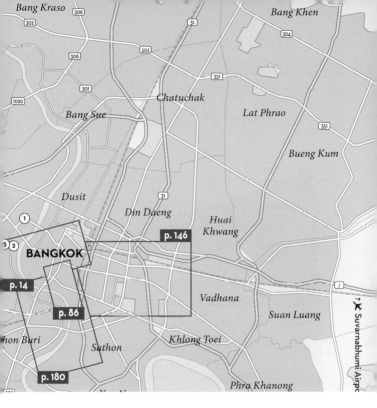

WAT SUAN SAWAN

A very well-hidden "abandoned" temple, probably Bangkok's most enigmatic religious site

Soi Charan Sanitwong 44, Bang Phlat

The Suan Sawan temple is tucked into the quiet alleyways north-east of Rama VIII Bridge. It is so well-hidden, in fact, that many people (even in the immediate neighbourhood) seem to be unaware of its existence. Persistence is needed to get here, particularly since asking directions is almost certain to result in being directed towards the great sprawling riverside temple complex of nearby Wat Kharuhabodi. However, it is worth persisting, because Wat Suan Sawan is likely to be the most enigmatic religious site you will visit in Bangkok.

This crumbling, old temple is almost a total mystery. On the rare occasions it has been written about, it is usually said to be 200 years old and "abandoned". It is very likely, however, that *both* these facts are untrue: it is considerably older, and it is clear that it is still visited by at least a few devotees. This second fact is particularly interesting since when you step inside (the door is always open) you will see the unmistakable signs of recent offerings and half-burned incense candles, yet even neighbours in the surrounding houses will tell you adamantly that nobody ever visits.

Experts estimate from its style that the temple was built in the late Ayutthaya Period (probably around 270 years ago), but it was very likely renovated about a century later during the reign of Rama III (1824 to 1851) when nearby Wat Kharuhabodi was under construction. More recently, Wat Suan Sawan has fallen into serious disrepair.

The large Buddha image on the main altar was probably originally gilded, but the gold has long since flaked off (or been removed), and the Buddha is now covered only with a layer of black lacquer. In this fervently Buddhist city, it is rare that a temple is allowed to fall into ruin, but the rickety condition of the roof tiles and the cracks that snake up the stucco walls are unmistakable signs that, unless something is done very soon, this wonderfully evocative old temple could be on its last legs. Take a chance to see it while you can, and simply sit quietly and soak up the atmosphere in solitude.

SIRIRAJ BIMUKSTHAN MUSEUM

Dive deeper into old Bangkok

2 Wanglang Road, Bangkok Noi
sirirajmuseum.com
Wednesday to Monday 10am–5pm

Siriraj Hospital, the oldest in Thailand, was founded in 1887 when Prince Siriraj, the 18-month-old son of Rama V, died from dysentery. There are now six medicine related museums in the hospital complex. The Parasitology and Medical museums, in particular, are known for their macabre exhibits – including preserved babies with various deformities, and the scrotum of a man who had elephantiasis – but on the western bank of the Chao Phraya River there is one that is a lot gentler on the stomach.

For those interested in the early years of Bangkok, the extensive Siriraj Bimuksthan Museum is well worth a visit. Its information-packed exhibits trace the history of the Thonburi area (including the re-routing of the Chao Phraya River, see p. 196), as well as that of traditional medicine, and the evolution of modern medicine in Thailand.

Just behind the museum an elegant glass corridor protects the excavated foundations of a palace and fort built during the Thonburi Era. They were found during an archaeological dig that revealed another treasure: the remains of a 24-metre-long teak and ironwood boat, which has been reconstructed and is now on display in the museum. Historians believe it may have been abandoned in what was then the dockyard of King Pinklao (see box, below).

The museum is housed in a striking red-brick building that opened in 1903 as the Bangkok Noi railway station – it was also the operations and supply base for the Japanese when they built the Burma Railway (known as the Death Railway) during World War II. The station has been moved 900 metres up the Bangkok Noi canal (see p. 126), but one steam locomotive remains, a tribute to this building's past.

The first Second King of Thailand

Prince Chatumani (1808–1866) was the younger brother of Prince Mongkut (see p. 72 and p. 237). As the sons of Rama II, both princes had an equally legitimate claim to the throne, but because Mongkut was older, he was crowned Rama IV in 1851 when their half-brother, Rama III, passed away. Rama IV did something never seen before in the history of Siam: he bestowed upon his younger brother the title of Second King, creating a rank equivalent to his own. Chatumani became King Pinklao, and had his own army and navy. He died before Rama IV and never ruled Siam, but he played a valuable role in establishing and maintaining important foreign relations.

LOCOMOTIVE GARAGE AT THONBURI STATION

A collection of historic iron workhorses

Thonburi Station, Siri Rat, Bangkok Noi

Steam train enthusiasts are in for a real treat at Thonburi Railway Station: there, in an old warehouse, stand five steam engines manufactured in the 1930s.

To get to the railway depot you will need to navigate across relatively busy tracks, but once there you will have the freedom to look around and get up close to the engines. The depot is a workshop for diesel locomotives, and there will be banging and clattering as mechanics tend to the workhorses – the C56 engines, however, are likely to be unattended (see p. 124 and p. 140 for other steam engines in Bangkok).

Class C56 trains were built by Japanese Government Railways between 1936 and 1939, and of the 164 locomotives built in this class, 93 were sent to the Asian countries occupied by Japan during World War II. By 1977 Thailand had phased out the use of steam engines, and the magnificent old C56s now only run on special ceremonial days, such as the king's birthday, when they shunt up the line to the ancient Siamese capital, Ayutthaya.

Look out for locomotive C56 15. Late every November it hauls a train 130 km west to Kanchanaburi for the annual River Kwai Bridge Festival, which pays tribute to the tens of thousands of workers who lost their lives while constructing what came to be known as the "Death Railway". The 415-km-long Thai–Burma railway line was built by civilian labourers and Allied prisoners of war in the early 1940s, and C56 31, a "classmate" of C56 15, was the very first locomotive to run on this line. It operated during and after World War II, and was eventually retired to Japan, where the locomotive is on display in a museum alongside the Yasukuni Shrine, which commemorates Japanese nationals who died during World War II.

Decoding the numbers

Every locomotive has its own identification number, and the steam engines in Thailand are classified according to a Japanese system as that is where they were manufactured. Take, for example, C56 15: the letter "C" indicates that the locomotive has three driving axles; "56" shows that it is a tender locomotive (numbers 10 to 49 are tank locomotives, and 50 to 99 are tender locomotives); and the third number in the sequence – 15 in this example – is the locomotive's running number.

BAAN BU BRONZEWORKING COMMUNITY

④

Where traditional handcrafted bronze bowls are made

133 Charansantiwong Soi 32, Siri Rat, Bangkok Noi

Along the Bangkok Noi canal there is a neighbourhood that dates back to the founding days of Bangkok. Baan Bu is a community of bronzeworkers who have been making beautiful stone-polished bronze bowls for about 240 years, and it is a wonderful area to explore and catch a glimpse of times and traditions past.

The shiny bronze bowls made here used to be an essential part of everyday life because they were used to cool water or store rice, or as alms bowls by monks (see p. 82). People no longer use these bowls in everyday life, and in order to keep the small industry alive, the Baan Bu artisans now also make tableware, which is usually given as wedding gifts.

The number of people working with this traditional craft is dwindling. Two hundred years ago almost every house in Baan Bu would have been producing the stone-polished bowls, but these days the only place where you can see the process – called *khan long hin* – is the Jiam Sangsajja Bronze Factory. Do not be fooled by the word "factory", however, as there is no slick machine production here: it is a basic workshop where hard-working people have honed their skills over generations.

The silky, smooth sheen of the polished metal exudes a luxurious quality that belies the six labour-intensive processes necessary to create the bowls. After melting copper, tin and gold, the processes involve intense heat, coals and rigorous pounding with hammers until the bowl has its basic shape. It is then cooled, hammered again and filed, before a design is etched by hand. Only then can the bowl be polished. The traditional method of rubbing a stone covered with coconut oil has now been replaced by polishing machines. It is exceptionally hard work in extreme conditions, and it can take six people four days to create eight large bronze bowls.

The bronzeworkers settled together in Baan Bu because Rama I wanted to model his new capital on Ayutthaya, where people lived in communities that centred on a particular skill – for example, a community that made firecrackers, or Buddha images, or turmeric powder. Very few of these communities remain.

The little lanes of the Baan Bu neighbourhood are interesting to explore. There is a traditional pharmacy that is almost a century old, as well as small shops selling hand-hammered stainless steelware and a small market.

WAT CHALAW

*One of the most outstanding architectural
undertakings ever attempted in Thailand*

Bang Kruai, Nonthaburi
Daily 8am–5.30pm

The Royal Barges Museum is a popular tourist destination, and visitors go to see the intricately carved vessels that are an exquisite tribute to Thai art and craftsmanship. Unbeknown to most of these visitors, just over 5 km away there is another barge that is just as extraordinary as the ones ridden in by Thai kings.

Wat Chalaw (often also written Wat Chalo) is a temple that stands on the 12-metre-wide "deck" of a 90-metre-long "barge" in sleepy Bang Kruai village. The concrete boat is modelled on the most coveted vessel at the Royal Barges Museum, the 46-metre-long *Suphannahong* (Golden Swan), which was carved from a single piece of teak in 1911. As with the *Suphannahong*, the bow of the concrete barge resembles a mythical swan.

The barge at Wat Chalaw, which has been described as "one of the most outstanding architectural undertakings ever attempted in Thailand", is surrounded by a moat that gives the impression the vessel is floating. There has been a temple in this location for half a millennia, but the barge temple was built in 1984 at a cost of several million dollars, despite the fact that much of the labour was undertaken by the devoted people of Bang Kruai.

It is not easy to find Wat Chalaw, and as you drive down Bang Kruai–Sai Noi Road you are likely to think that you are many miles from any impressive landmark. Until, that is, you arrive under the looming bowsprit of what seems to be a golden ship stranded above the Bangkok Noi canal.

To get here, take the express boat to Nonthaburi Pier, cross the river by ferry and take a motorbike or *songthaew* (the pickup-truck taxis that are known literally as "two rows") for about 15 minutes to Bang Kruai. Once at the temple you will see a small footbridge across the moat that leads you to a door giving access to the upper deck. There is a delightfully peaceful and ornate meditation hall where the wheelhouse would be on a real ship.

A mechanised robot for donations to supply poor families with free coffins

Wat Chalaw offers an unusual possibility to make merit by making donations to supply poor families with free coffins for their deceased (see p. 154). Unusually, however, at Wat Chalaw this service is advertised by a mechanised robot of a skeleton in sunglasses. He might be the first thing you will notice, eerily bowing his bony *wai* towards you when you arrive in the temple car park.

WAT PRASAT

⑥

Meet the female spirits of Bangkok's most haunted temple

18 Bang Kruai – Sai Noi Road, Nonthaburi

Few Thais would risk talking about the ghost of Wat Prasat within earshot of the temple: "If she hears people talking about her, she'll follow them home and haunt them," they explain. Apparently, the ghost of Wat Prasat does not understand English – so if you have an English-speaking guide who is brave enough, they might whisper that this site is protected by the spirit of a royal lady, sometimes called Usawadee-Tewi.

Usawadee-Tewi is quick to punish anyone who behaves without due respect. Such acts of "disrespect" included a plan to turn the area into a residential complex, and it is said that when the pile-drivers were brought in to begin the foundations, it was impossible for them even to penetrate the ground. The project was abandoned, but neighbours are doubtful that anyone would have wanted to live on Bangkok's most haunted land, anyway.

Usawadee-Tewi's oversized spirit-house stands in a prominent position by the roadside, but she is not the only powerful female spirit in residence here. In a small compound at the western edge of the temple complex, you will find an eerie little shrine decorated with offerings of miniature dolls, baby clothes, plastic toys and false fingernails. Next to this lies a 39-metre-long tree trunk which is said to be more than 1,000 years old.

A spirit called Nang Ta-khian (Lady of the Tree) inhabits this trunk.

Despite being valuable hardwood, *Hopea odorata* (to give the tree its Latin name) was traditionally protected in Thailand because it was said that the spirit of the tree would haunt whoever felled it. The Lady of the Tree is often said to haunt houses if the beams or stilts are made from this type of wood, but it is considered safe to use in monasteries since the power of the monks could protect them.

Aside from the courageous monks, few Thais would risk setting foot near Wat Prasat after dark. "I don't think there are really any ghosts here these days," smiled one stall-holder who sells drinks to the few visitors who come to the temple, "but we always make sure we're gone long before dark, just in case."

KOH SARN CHAO NEIGHBOURHOOD

An historic "rural" neighbourhood

Wat Champa
22 Phutthamonthon Sai 1 Road, Taling Chan

On the outskirts of Bangkok there is a neighbourhood that predates the city itself: the Kho Sarn Chao canal community can trace its roots back 500 years, to the middle period of the Ayutthaya Era. The community, which is completely surrounded by two canals, is a living museum. Koh Sarn Chao is a quiet, leafy neighbourhood connected by a network of footpaths that cover the narrow canals. Many of the traditional-style houses are fringed with carefully carved wooden details along the roofs and verandas, and are dwarfed by the trees that have grown along the canals for generations. The island bursts with fruit trees, and the produce is sold at nearby markets.

Wat Champa, the temple central to this community, was restored during the reign of Rama II (1809 to 1824), but built when Ayutthaya was still the powerhouse of Siam. It is interesting to find the unusual details in Chinese porcelain and elaborately carved wood that decorate the buildings.

Close to the temple is Baan Song Butree, a beautiful house built to honour the artistic heritage of the family that lives there. It is owned by the community chairman, Thaweesak Wangchan, who invites visitors to step through the oval-shaped doorway into his canal-side home. One of the buildings is private, and the one open to the public is decorated with carved doors and vintage furniture, and old portraits of the previous king. From upstairs there is a view down onto the canals, offering a peek into life on the water.

Thaweesak is working hard to keep the dying art of *tang yuak* alive. *Tang yuak* are intricately carved decorations that are made from the soft centre of banana trees and used to decorate coffins for cremation ceremonies – usually for members of the royal family, or esteemed monks.

Another traditional craft being kept alive on this island is the making of *pang puang*, the perfumed powder garlands made to worship Buddha statues, or to decorate hair pins.

To keep their traditions alive and prevent their historic neighbourhood from being torn down, over the past decade the Koh Sarn Chao community has navigated that careful balance between inviting tourists onto their island, while maintaining their authenticity. Information boards have been put up along the canals, giving insights into the history and traditions of the area.

HOUSE OF MUSEUMS

A delightful collection of retro memorabilia

170/17 Moo 7, Soi 2, Khlong Pho Road, Thung Kru
Saturday and Sunday 10am–5pm

The House of Museums is a place that sparks curiosity and delight. Rather than "just" a museum, it is an enchanting complex of rooms that contain recreations of shops and small businesses from the 1960s, and they are all packed with fascinating collections of toys, trinkets and everyday objects. The museum was founded by Anake Nawigamune, a writer who has published hundreds of articles and booklets on Thai history, culture and travel. In the 1990s Nawigamune, who enjoyed collecting old items as a child, found himself frustrated when researching old toys and costumes – there was no central place where they were collected or displayed. In a newspaper article about the museum, which is now framed and hanging on a wall there, Nawigamune is quoted as saying, "I often got stuck when I wrote my history books. There was little evidence left to study. Pictures were especially rare." It was because of this that Nawigamune reached out to other collectors, and set out to establish a museum, one that would house "ordinary", everyday objects from yesteryear.

The result is captivating: the museum exhibits Thai urban life predominantly during the 1960s and 1970s, and anyone who enjoys retro styles or taking nostalgic walks down memory lane will be enthralled here. The collections include books, toys, magazines, miniature cars, toothpaste tubes, pencils, telephones, books, games, cards, cameras, suitcases, and matchboxes. There is not much information available in English, but that does not matter – the intrigue is the objects themselves.

Within the museum there is a general trading store, a toy shop, a traditional medicine shop, a dental clinic and a souvenir shop (which has many old-fashioned toys and trinkets for sale), as well as a goldsmith's, a record store, an old classroom and an old coffee shop – and that is just on the ground floor. Among the displays upstairs are a small cinema (look for the photographs of Thai film legend Mitr Chaibancha – see p. 148), a barber shop, a printing press and an old kitchen. Look, too, for the old "fortune-telling machines", where those who wanted to know their future would slip a coin into a slot, and a pre-written message would be delivered.

THAI FILM MUSEUM

An entertaining tribute to the film industry

94 Phutthamonthon Sai 5 Road, Phutthamonthon
fapot.org/en/museum.php
Tuesday to Sunday 10am–5pm

A t Bangkok's city limits there is a quirky museum that celebrates the industry that contributes more than US$2.2 billion to the Thai economy annually: film.

A visit to the museum feels like being on a film set: sculptures of studio lights, an old camera dolly, and grip equipment are scattered around replicas of buildings that played starring roles in the Thai and international film industries. There is New York City's iconic Nickleodeon cinema; Paris's Grand Café, where the world's first movie screening was shown in 1895; and the Prince Alangkarn Theatre, where the first movie was shown in Bangkok, two years later.

There is also a replica of Black Maria, the world's first motion picture studio, and bronze statues of film-making pioneers George Eastman and Thomas Alva Edison. Around the museum, life-size sculptures pay homage to other great film personalities, and in one of the ponds there are sculptures of actors and cameramen shooting a scene from *His Sweet Melody*, a popular Thai musical filmed in 1937.

A highlight of this beautifully constructed museum is the tour that takes place inside the replica of the Prince Alangkarn Theatre. Pick up an audio guide from the office and be transported through various rooms displaying equipment and memorabilia from the film industry, and follow the development of the film production process. Pay particular attention to the set showing Thailand's favourite ghost, Mae Nak (see p. 172), and look out for the replica of Thai icon Mitr Chaibancha hanging from a helicopter (see p. 148).

Steam enthusiasts will be interested in the C56 locomotive engine (see p. 126) at the museum's entrance. The bronze figure at the front of the engine is Prince Purachatra Jayakara, a son of Rama V. The prince, who was the Commander of the Royal Siamese Railway, was an amateur film-maker, and in 1922 he founded the Topical Film Service of the Royal State Railways, a production centre for news and documentary films that is considered to be the foundation of film production in Thailand.

The bespectacled figure standing in front of the Prince Alangkarn Theatre replica is Prince Thongthaem Sambassatra, a younger brother of Rama V. The prince, who is said to have brought cameras and film-making equipment back from Europe in 1897, is considered to be the country's first film-maker and the Father of Thai Cinema.

THAI HUMAN IMAGERY MUSEUM

"Baldy-butting" – and other bizarre aspects of Thai life

43/2 Mu 1, Pinklao Nakhon Chaisi Road, Khun Kaeo, Nakhon Chai Si
Monday to Friday 9am–5.30pm; Saturday and Sunday 8.30am–6pm

When a place has a name as dry as "Thai Human Imagery Museum", you would hardly expect to encounter anything quirky. But when it comes to quirkiness, this museum is full of it.

In the Thai Folk Culture section, for example, there is a full-size village scene that sheds light on the rural sport of "baldy-butting". The rules were apparently not complicated – two bald men had to butt heads, and the first to bleed was declared the loser. Apparently, the last official tournament of the gladiatorial sport took place in Petchburi in 1994, but this "sport" was a relatively common event in many rural communities. It would seem to be a pastime that is at odds with the typically peaceful and good-natured Thai people, but this museum contains several unexpected exhibits that might make you rethink what you thought you knew about Thailand.

Although it is normally described as a "waxwork museum" the life-size figures are actually made of fibreglass (due to the Thai climate), with every line in every face meticulously engraved and each strand of hair implanted individually – even on the two life-size horses in the lobby. The faces are realistic, and in many cases the expressions are powerfully heart-rending, especially in the intensely poignant historical sections portraying slavery and human trafficking.

One of the first rooms you enter is a mock-up of a modern-day sitting room with a group of Thai men hunched over a chess board, with two other men dozing on a sofa in the corner. The overall effect is so eerily realistic that you almost feel like an intruder.

There is much in this museum that is likely to surprise you. Folk heroes in the form of musicians, poets and playwrights are brought to life, and unexpectedly, there are likenesses of just three non-Thais: Lincoln, Gandhi and Churchill. You can take photos of all them along with about 30 particularly revered monks and abbots.

While Thai visitors are allowed to snap pictures in the rooms dedicated to the former monarchs of the Chakri Dynasty, there is a sign prohibiting photography for foreigners in the royal rooms. it explains that some disrespectful tourists made rude gestures in their selfies and posted them on social media "causing scandal to the royal family".

JESADA TECHNIK MUSEUM

Paradise for petrol-heads

73120 Tambon Ngewrai, Nakhon Chai Sri
Tuesday to Sunday 9am–5pm

⑪

The hangar-sized Jesada Technik Museum is a veritable petrol-head paradise. There are enough quirky vehicles on display to make this a truly jaw-dropping experience, even for visitors with only a passing interest in motoring history.

Thai businessman Jesada Dejsakulrit has been collecting vehicles for about 30 years, and his private collection now includes more than 300 rare and classic cars, and about 200 motorbikes and scooters. He clearly has a soft-spot for bubble cars, and for many, the stars of the show are the diminutive egg-shaped three-wheel 1960s BMWs and Messerschmitts. Try not to trip over the tiny red Peel – the smallest production car ever made. (One of these recently fetched US$175,000 at an auction in Florida.)

Next to the bubble cars there is an entire fleet of what appear to be leather-covered cars: they are Czechoslovakian Verolex Oskars, which were made throughout the 1950s, and were covered in brown vinyl. From the same decade there are a couple of astoundingly well-preserved Amphicars – the sort of car-boat combos that James Bond would have appreciated. There is even a highly unusual little car with a steering wheel and controls at both ends, for driving either forwards or backwards.

The cars from the 1930s and 1940s are mostly in serviceable (if not showroom) condition. For sheer eye-candy look out for the old Fords, Humbers, Citroens, Studebakers, Mercedes, a yellow New York cab and two stretch Checkers limousines. The collection is highly eclectic with even a double-decker London bus, a helicopter and a couple of hovercrafts thrown into the mix. Dejsakulrit once even bought a Russian "Whiskey Class" submarine, but it sank while being towed to Thailand. Motoring aficionados will appreciate a retro gem in the form of a 1980s DMC DeLorean (à la *Back to the Future*) – and the 1993 Maserati sitting unassumingly near the back corner might be one of the unsung stars of the collection.

In another dustier (and rustier) part of the warehouse, there is an entire collection of cycle-trishaws, bicycles, motorised cycles, and more classic Vespas and Lambrettas than you are likely to ever see under one roof. This almost unknown museum might be the most startling private collection of vehicles in the world, but according to the staff, none of the vehicles here are for sale, and there is not even an admission fee.

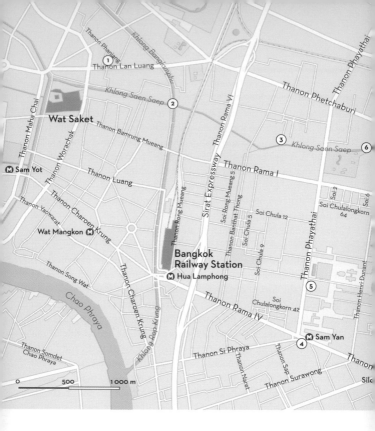

East Bangkok

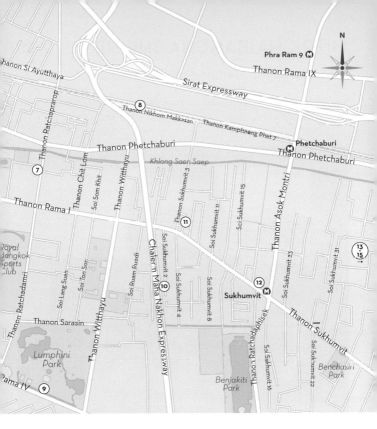

MITR CHAIBANCHA SHRINE

A memorial for Thailand's most-loved actor

Wat Sunthon Thammathan, Phaniang Road, Pom Prap Sattru Phai
Daily 6am–6pm

The remains of Thailand's favourite film star, Mitr Chaibancha (1934–1970), are held at Wat Sunthon Thammathan. Mitr was exceptionally popular during the golden age of Thai cinema in the 1960s. At that time the Thai film industry was producing up to 100 16 mm films per year. Mitr starred in almost half of these films – during his 15-year career he featured in about 350 films and sometimes worked on three films in one day.

As a child, Mitr lived close to this temple, in the Nang Loeng neighbourhood (named after the Mon word for the large clay jars once produced here). It is estimated that 100,000 people filled the streets during the pre-cremation rituals, and reports say that Wat Sunthon Thammathan was damaged by the sheer volume of people who had come to pay their respects.

Take a walk around the temple and it is soon obvious where the remains of the actor have been laid to rest: a photograph of the dapper star is surrounded by a large wreath of plastic flowers. Just outside the temple complex, alongside the gate and in a small room watched over by a monk, offerings of flowers and incense are made to the larger-than-life-size bust of the actor, which is covered with gold leaf and surrounded by flowers and framed photographs.

Mitr, who had trained as a pilot and worked as a flight instructor at the Don Mueng Royal Thai Airforce Base, died during an accident while filming *Inseethong* (*Golden Eagle*). He was dangling from a rope ladder that hung from a low-flying helicopter when he fell to his death. The plan had been to film Mitr at a low altitude, and then use a stunt double for the second shot, with the helicopter flying at a higher altitude (this scene – moments before the accident – has been recreated at the Thai Film Museum, see p. 140). It was the final scene of the film, which was released four years after the accident.

A career ended by long hours spent under bright lights on filmsets – or having to cry so often during filming?

Actress Petchara Chaowarat (b. 1943), also an icon of the 1960s, starred in about 300 films, and worked alongside Mitr in about half of them. Her last film was released in 1979, when she was forced to end her acting career due to very bad eyesight. It is suspected that her sight deteriorated due to long hours spent under bright lights on filmsets (and, some say, having to cry so often during filming).

BRIDGE AT BOBAE MARKET

Where James Bond-like stunts happen every day

Where Krung Kasem Road crosses Saen Saep Canal, Pom Prap Sattru Phai
Khlong boats operate weekdays 5.30am– 8.30pm; weekends 5.30am–7pm
Boat fare is between 10 baht and 20 baht, depending on distance

In the 1974 film *The Man with the Golden Gun* there is an iconic chase scene where James Bond tears down a Bangkok *khlong* (canal), pulling all sorts of death-defying stunts to avoid obstacles. For many Bangkok commuters, this sort of experience is just part of the normal routine of an everyday trip to work. Your first inkling of this might come after buying a ticket at Phanfa Bridge (near Wat Saket, see p. 26, p. 28 and p. 30) when you notice that the ticket collectors on Saen Saep Canal commuter boats are kitted out, stuntman style, with crash-helmets. Be prepared for the moment when the needle-like boat squeezes itself flat – like a clamping oyster-shell – as the boat slides under a low bridge. The boats are equipped with a nifty mechanical lever that allows the skipper to collapse the roof over the passengers' heads when the water level is high.

Most visitors limit themselves to the section of the river that runs between Phanfa Bridge and Hua Chang Pier (next to Jim Thompson's House). The 11 baht ticket-price must make this one of the world's most inexpensive and exciting boat trips, and it is certainly worth exploring farther along Saen Saep Canal (see p. 158).

There are several low bridges along the *khlong*, but the one at Bobae Market is the lowest, and therefore the best place to watch Bangkok's own James Bond riverboats pull their unique shrinking manoeuvre.

James Bond stunts in Bangkok

The famous James Bond boat-chase was filmed at Damnoen Saduak Floating Market in 1974, long before that location became such a logjam that even Bond would be unable to pick up any speed. The *Guinness Book of Records* lists the first astro spiral motorcar stunt as being filmed in Bangkok for that same film, where the American stuntman, Loren "Bumps" Willert, pulled off the legendary stunt in an AMC Hornet X. The car retired to the National Motor Museum in England, but it is a shame that it did not end up closer to its old stomping grounds at the wonderful Jesada Teknik Museum (see p. 144).

SILK WEAVERS
OF BAAN KRUA NUA

Where the Jim Thompson silk story began

Baan Krua Nua, Saen Saep, Ratchathewi
Weekdays 9am–5.30pm; weekends and holidays 8.30am–6pm

Thai silk has become synonymous with the legend of Jim Thompson, the American entrepreneur who revived the country's silk industry in the 1950s. While his exquisite teak house, now a museum, is a popular destination in Bangkok, the community that sparked Thompson's interest in silk has all but been forgotten.

Baan Krua Nua, just over the canal from Thompson's house, is where descendants of the Cham ethnic group from southern Laos and Cambodia settled in the 1780s. The community were highly skilled weavers, and it was when he stumbled upon a small workshop here that Thompson's business plan began to take shape. He took samples of the silk cloth woven here to New York and, as Thompson's silk business flourished, it was the Baan Krua Nua weavers who supplied him with fabrics.

Each piece of beautiful handwoven textile created in Baan Krua Nua is unique. They source the raw materials in Surin, in north-east Thailand, and then prepare, dye and weave the silk in workshops that have hardly changed since Thompson first poked his head in almost 70 years ago.

Wearing a 1970s-style silk shirt and aviator sunglasses, silk producer Mr Ud looks very much like a silk magnate himself, but the glory days are very likely over for the silk weaving community of Baan Krua Nua. When Thompson's nephew took over the company, he set up a factory elsewhere, and Mr Ud's family is now one of only two that remain in their traditional business. His workshop is too small to sell silk to the Jim Thompson company, Mr Ud says. Mr Ud's neighbour, Loong Aood, is more fortunate. With four old handlooms, his slightly larger workshop still supplies small quantities to the company that the "King of Silk" founded in 1950. Hanging on a wall at Aood Bankrua Thai Silk there is a photograph of Aood as a teenager standing beside a very dapper looking Jim Thompson. Aood says he met Thompson when he was six years old, and that he was 15 when Thompson disappeared.

The king of silk

The story of Jim Thompson (1906–1967) is one of the most enduring myths of post-WWII Bangkok. The mysterious tale of an ex-spy (maybe) who was a part-owner of the Oriental Hotel and became a silk magnate before disappearing in Malaysia's Cameron Highlands in 1967 is almost the stuff of legend. Several books have been written about him, and in 2001 the film *Jim Thompson: Silk King* was released.

COFFIN DONATIONS
AT WAT HAU LAMPHONG

Gift a coffin for a better afterlife

Wat Hau Lamphong, 728 Rama IV Road, Bang Rak

Among the many ways Thais make merit for the next life (see p. 19), sponsoring a coffin might be the most unexpected. Next to a little Chinese-style shrine at the northern edge of Wat Hau Lamphong, the Ruamkatanyu Foundation runs a charity that allows worshippers (and visitors) the chance to do just that: to sponsor a coffin for someone whose family cannot afford to buy one themselves. (You can also sponsor a coffin at Wat Chalaw, see p. 130, where the initiative is bizarrely advertised by a mechanical skeleton wearing sunglasses.)

You can donate any amount, but 500 baht is enough to pay for a coffin and shroud. Donors fill out a pink form known as a "merit slip" and take it to an attendant at one of the desks who, after accepting the donation, hands over a "value certificate". The donor then takes the merit slip into the back room where they pray before gluing the slip onto one of the white-washed wooden coffins stacked in the room. They then take the value certificate into the little temple and set it alight in one of the oil burners, taking care to drop it safely into a big brass bowl so that it burns completely away. Next, the donor hits a drum in the corner three times, then gives three taps to each of the three bronze bells and, finally, *wais* (hands together in supplication) in front of each of the deities in the temple.

According to some, the bells and drums are a way to emphasise your merit-making deed more effectively to the gods. When you consider the cost of funerals (and the cultural pressure involved in securing a ceremony worthy of family members), many would agree that it is in any case a laudable cause.

Regardless of religious affiliation, foreign visitors are welcome to go through the offering performance. For many it represents a unique experience and a very unusual way to give a little back to the country. There is an attendant in the shrine who will be happy to guide you through the process, but you would be expected to gain a little extra merit by tipping him.

Until recently one could also make merit at Wat Hau Lamphong by buying food for the herd of sacred cows (and even buffalo) that lived here. According to temple staff the sacred bovines have been moved to another temple near Lop Buri where, it is to be hoped, the grass might be somewhat greener.

MUSEUM OF
IMAGING TECHNOLOGY

⑤

A secret haven for photography purists

Faculty of Science, Chulalongkorn University, 254 Phayathai Road, Pathum Wan
Note: Access is via a back stairway in the Faculty of Science
Monday to Friday 10am–3pm

A quick glance at the visitor's book is ample proof that this truly remains a secret spot among Bangkok museums: in a busy week the grandly named Museum of Imaging Technology might see 10 visitors. Yet, for a photography enthusiast, Thailand's first photography museum is well worth focusing on.

This vibrant and colourful city (and Thailand in general) has become famous as a photographer's paradise. It is a fact that was greatly appreciated by the late King Bhumibol Adulyadej, Rama IX, many of whose countless portraits show a beloved Canon strung around his neck. In fact, this museum was created under the patronage of the king's elder sister, Princess Galyani Vadhana, and the main attraction is a display case of cameras that were owned by the royal family.

While the royal family have traditionally been dedicated Canon aficionados, the most spectacular camera in this case is a limited edition 1984 Nikon FA Gold. Covered with 24-carat-gold plating (even down to the logo on the lens-cap!) and shrouded in lizard skin, these models sell for around US$12,000.

Unusually well-written information boards (in English) take you from the earliest days of photographic history. You start with the discovery of the spectrum of the colours that make up sunlight and the very first photograph (taken by Joseph Nicéphore Niepce in 1826). From there you pass through the dark arts of daguerreotypes, calotypes (the first negative-positive imagery) and into the explosive intricacies of shooting on wet plates and dry plates. There is nostalgia in the lost world of 110 mm and 35 mm film and those psychedelic filter collections (starbursts, soft-focus, fake rainbows, sunsets) that filled camera bags through the 1970s and 1980s.

Take time to wander among a wealth of information – there are details of the Russian camera industry, the history of Leica, Nikon, Kodak and, of course, Canon. A separate room is dedicated to a space-age "Canon Exploratorium" – strangely reminiscent of the flight deck of a 1970s cinematic rocket-ship. The fact that the interactive displays in this room seem to be permanently out of order is perhaps fitting: after all, this is a museum aimed at dedicated photographic purists and it barely deigns even to recognise the digital revolution.

Cruise Thailand's longest canal

Central Bangkok
Commuter boats run daily 7.30am–3pm

S aen Saep is the longest *khlong* (canal) in Thailand, yet very few visitors take the time to explore even a fraction of the 72-km-long waterway, which stretches from the Banglamphu Canal (see p. 22) east to the Bang Pakong River, about a third of the way from Bangkok to Cambodia.

As one of Bangkok's main arteries, Saen Saep has been transporting cargo and people since it was built by Muslim workers in 1837 to transport arms and weapons during a conflict with Vietnam. Now, more than 100,000 commuters use the canal daily, and it is regularly used by travellers who tend to board a commuter boat at Phanfa Bridge (near the Golden Mount) and then explore only as far as Hua Chang Pier (for access to the Jim Thompson House Museum). Once in a while, an intrepid traveller might visit the Muslim silk-weaving community of Baan Krua Nua (see p. 152) on the northern bank of the canal.

Asok Boat Pier lies about halfway along the entire boat route, and feels like the boundary between modern Bangkok city and the outlying suburbs. When the Scandinavian explorer and writer Carl Bock arrived in Bangkok in 1881, there were brothel-boats on the canal near Asok, and "punters" would be rowed out into midstream here – one of the widest sections of the canal – for the duration of their tryst.

The brothel boats are long gone, and these days passenger boats barely run a third of the canal's total distance, but the ride to the last (most easterly) of the boat's 28 stops at Sriboonreung Temple Pier takes about an hour and constitutes a voyage into a part of Bangkok that is almost unknown to outsiders. It is the end of an era for many of Bangkok's *khlong*-side communities, and more and more of the venerable old teak buildings are disappearing with each year. You can see a part of Bangkok life that is known only to a few simply by voyaging up the canal, but if you take the time to disembark, you will find that the walkways running along Saen Saep's banks offer an unforgettable opportunity to become better acquainted with some of the last of Bangkok's traditional canal-side communities.

The long, narrow commuter boats that run on the canal today make for a thrilling, rollercoaster ride. They are uniquely fitted with collapsing roofs that fall flat when the skipper pulls a special lever (see p. 150).

TRIMURTI SHRINE

⑦

Pray for romance at the Lovers' Shrine

Central World, 999/9 Rama I Road, Pathum Wan
Busiest on Thursday evenings around 9.30pm

With a veritable armada of buses, taxis, tuk-tuks and motorbikes belching their fumes along the great concrete canyon of Ratchadamri Road, it might appear incongruous that the Trimurti Shrine is fronted with a sign warning worshippers to "refrain from lighting candles and incense sticks since the smoke may be hazardous to health". Trimurti Shrine is better known as Lovers' Shrine, and it is doubtful whether the romantics who come here ever spare a thought for their lungs. This location is all about the heart.

The Trimurti Shrine honours the trinity of the Hindu deities: Brahma (the creator), Vishnu (the preserver) and Shiva (the destroyer). Perhaps it is this symbolic union that has prompted people to consider the deities here *the* spiritual authorities on relationships and romance – or perhaps it is the urban legend that in the past, young women who have prayed here have met the men of their dreams.

While people make offerings of roses, candles and red Fanta throughout the week, it is busiest on Thursday evenings around 9.30pm – it is said that this is when the gods descend to Earth and is therefore a good time to ask for their blessing. An offering of nine red roses or nine red candles is thought to garner the best results, and worshippers here must bear in mind that once the wish is made and the blessing given, they must continue to make regular offerings lest the romance wain. (Those looking for a good love-match sometimes pray at a shrine at Wat Mahabut, see p. 172.)

The ornate white Trimurti Shrine, which houses the image of a gold-coloured human body with two heads, is almost 8 metres high. The replica of a 16th-century statue from Ayutthaya stands on a smooth tiled platform that sometimes shimmers with water.

The Trimurti Shrine is one of six Hindu shrines on Ratchaprasong Square. The first one erected was the famous Erawan Shrine, built in 1956 to appease spirits on the land on which the Erawan Hotel had been built. The spiritual power of this shrine was said to have been so strong that when Central World was built in 1990, the Trimurti Shrine was erected as a counterforce, and as the area developed, shrines to other Hindu gods were placed outside newly erected buildings. The Ratchadamri intersection is now sometimes called the "Intersection of the Gods".

THAI LABOUR MUSEUM

Poignant insight into the "Dignity of Labour"

503/20 Nikhom Makkasan Road, Makkasan, Ratchathewi
Wednesday to Sunday 10am–4.30pm

Much has been written about the long-suffering Thai farmers and the harsh realities of rural life, but the Thai Labour Museum is a must-see for anyone who wants to understand the struggles of urban labourers in Bangkok. The displays lead you through six fascinating rooms on the often-disturbing journey that Thai workers have made – and are still making – towards something approaching fairer treatment.

The museum follows the history of Thai workers from the era of slavery, including the 1700s and 1800s, when indentured workers called *phrai* were forced to work without pay for feudal leaders (see p. 112). Slavery was abolished in Siam in 1908, and most of the exhibits in this museum focus on more recent times and specific branches of the economy (heavy industry, textiles, transport, construction and even kickboxing) and the problems faced by the human workhorses in those fields.

One memorable section deals with the Kader factory fire, the worst industrial accident in Thai history in which 188 workers (mostly women) died: these deaths were chiefly attributed to bad architecture and non-existent safety-precautions. The fact that the factory was producing toys for export – toys that the impoverished workers could never have afforded for their own children – made the case even more heart-breaking. Some of the charred toys form a particularly haunting part of the display. Another section deals with the sweatshops where under-aged children are forced to work in dangerous, cramped and poorly ventilated conditions for extremely poor wages. Although it sounds very intense, the museum makes for a highly educational visit, and at times when dealing with lighter topics, it is even entertaining.

A monument at the front of this building (which served as police station and railway union office before it became a museum in 1993) portrays a man and a woman working together to push an oversized gearwheel forward. The monument is called "The Dignity of Labour" but the museum itself shows that more than a century after slavery was abolished, this dignity is all too often nothing but a fallacy.

A compulsory visit

The Thai Labour Museum should be considered a compulsory visit (along with the Anti-Corruption Museum – see p. 222) for anyone who is considering working in Thailand, or for anyone who truly wants to understand the country.

MONITOR LIZARDS AT LUMPHINI PARK

The real-life dragons of Lumphini Park

Lumphini Park, Rama IV Road, Pathum Wan
Daily 5am–9pm

"**B**eware: here be dragons" was traditionally engraved on the Asia charts of ancient mariners. It is not the sort of warning you would expect on a map of modern Bangkok, but it might as well be there: the monitor lizards that prowl the waterways of Lumphini Park are almost the size of Komodo dragons, the creatures that inspired those words on old maritime charts.

While you might see big monitor lizards in many of the city's canals, the best place to see Bangkok's most formidable dragons is by the little bridge at the south-western entrance to Lumphini Park since, until recently, vendors sold packages of food for people to feed the lizards as a way of making merit (see p. 19).

The Department of the Environment has estimated that some of the specimens in the park reach 3 metres long – falling just short of the 3.21-metre record-breaker that was recorded in Sri Lanka. The feeding of monitor lizards was prohibited in 2016 when the park's population surpassed 400. Female monitor lizards can lay 20 to 30 eggs up to three times each year. Attempts were made to control the population by relocating adults and destroying eggs. Few hatchlings reach maturity because the lizards are opportunistic cannibals, but the largest specimens you will see might be more than 20 years old.

Commonly known as the Asian water monitor (*Varanus salvator*), these powerful reptiles are equipped with serrated teeth and a bone-crushing bite that herpetologists claim is mildly venomous. Recent research has shown that monitor lizard venom contains the same toxin found in rattlesnakes. Although not timid, they are not considered vicious as they tend to keep their distance. There has never been a reported "attack" on a human, although cats and small dogs can be at risk ... and a few cyclists have been thrown from their bikes in collisions.

When insulting a monitor lizard can bring misfortune ...

The local name for the monitors, *hia*, has been corrupted into a powerful swear word in Thai, yet many people believe that insulting a monitor lizard can bring misfortune. In past times they would often even be honoured with such terms as "most noble golden dragon".

The debate is ongoing as to whether Lumphini Park's dragon population should be controlled and some see their presence in a highly optimistic light: "If a *hia* goes into someone's room, they'll become rich," one park employee explained.

THE ATLANTA HOTEL

(10)

A retro delight in Bangkok's commercial centre

78 Soi 2, Sukhumvit Road, Khlong Toei
theatlantahotelbangkok.com
Meals with music composed by Rama IX (open to hotel guests only) between
noon and 1pm

The Mandarin Oriental might be considered the grande dame of hotels in Bangkok, but The Atlanta Hotel has, quite likely, been more instrumental in shaping the modern Bangkok that many travellers realise today. With its wonderfully retro (and original) foyer, The Atlanta stands as a nostalgic tribute to the pioneering days of modern tourism in Bangkok.

Among its attributes, The Atlanta claims a number of Thai firsts: the first hotel with air-conditioned rooms; the first hotel pool and children's pool; the first hotel to provide in-house films for guests; and the first German restaurant. The hotel's founder was also the first private-yacht owner in Thailand.

The hotel foyer remains as it was in the early 1960s. The black and white checked floor, deep red walls, mosaicked columns, glass chandelier and red leatherette seating will thrill any traveller with a passion for nostalgia and an eye for design. Those with a penchant for literature will delight in trawling through the displays of books written by writers who have stayed at The Atlanta.

Founded in 1952, the hotel was already well established when, by the mid-1960s, thousands of American army troops stationed in Asia flocked to Bangkok for their R&R. It was during this time that massage parlours, go-go bars and cheap hotels sprung up; The Atlanta would have benefitted from the GI's dollars, but ever since the mid-1980s, any sordid behaviour at the hotel has been strictly off-limits. "Sex tourists not allowed" warns the large sign at the hotel entrance.

The Atlanta was established when Dr Max Henn, a German pharmacologist, opened the rooms above the laboratory of his pharmaceutical business for rent. Business was slow at the Atlanta Chemical Company, but the hospitality side flourished to such an extent that by the early 1960s Queen Rambai, the widow of Rama VII, was a regular patron of the restaurant.

The hotel's standards and ambiance later declined and, by the time Professor Charles Henn took ownership in 1986, its clientele were significantly less than genteel. Henn took it upon himself to restore the dignity of the hotel.

Have a meal to music composed by Rama IX

Between noon and 1pm, patrons with an ear for music will enjoy having their meals to music composed by Rama IX, which is played in the hotel's dining room (open to hotel guests only).

OI ARAB

The romance of the Middle East in the heart of Bangkok

Soi Sukhumvit 3–5, Watthana

Djellaba-wearing men and veiled woman flit between spice stores, gold stores, baklava bakeries and perfumeries. Flickering neon signs in Arabic script advertise the wares of the Thai-Iraqi Tour Company, the Arabian Dental Clinic and restaurants with names like Al Hussain, Yemeni Petra, Al-Andalus and Shahrazad (the latter being the oldest in the neighbourhood, having opened in 1983). An evening in Soi Arab is a chance to enjoy the atmosphere of Bangkok's own Arabic oasis.

It might be an exaggeration, but it has been said that a 300-metre stroll along Soi Arab offers a chance to take in much of what you might see on the 5,000-km-long Spice Trail from China to Persia and Arabia. It is hard to imagine you are right across the road from the red lights of notorious Nana Plaza, and after Nana's sleaziness the atmosphere here, in what is sometimes known as Arab Street or Arab Town, is a breath of fresh (or spicy) air. You will see relatively few Western tourists here, and the little quarter retains a sense of authenticity thanks to its popularity with Arab expats.

Soi Arab is a great place to shop for shoes, perfume, leather luggage, jewellery and watches (although beware of brand rip-offs). More than shopping, however, it is the food that will entice you to this area, but bear in mind that few establishments here serve alcohol. If you enjoy Arabic food, you will be spoiled for choice with Yemeni, Egyptian, Iraqi, Jordanian, Iranian and Pakistani restaurants enticing diners with regional specialities. The Nasir al-Masri restaurant-terrace has been one of the area's prime people-watching spots since it opened in 1986, and The Happy Yemen Restaurant is famous for its succulent lamb dishes ... and for selling naan breads the size of manhole covers!

In his book *Siamese Melting Pot: Ethnic Minorities in the Making of Bangkok* (Silkworm Books, 2017), Edward Van Roy estimates that in 1782 there were about 4,000 Arabs and Persians among Bangkok's population of 30,000. While many of the workers in Soi Arab might be relatively recent arrivals – including (as reported by Al Jazeera in 2018) many refugees from Pakistan, Syria and Iraq – the fascinating cultural mix combines to form what might be one of the most unexpectedly enticing nightlife areas in the city.

TERMINAL 21

Travel the world – in a mall like no other

88 Soi Sukhumvit 19, Watthana
terminal21.co.th
Daily 10am–10pm

Shopping is synonymous with a trip to Bangkok, and while trawling through the city's various markets is something every visitor should experience, there is no shortage of glitzy malls featuring high-end boutiques and designer brands, or shopping complexes offering discounted deals. Terminal 21, in the heart of the city, is a mall like no other and it is worth a visit, not so much for the shops, but simply for the mall itself – here you are just as likely to find yourself walking into one of London's Underground stations, as you are navigating a maze of streets in Tokyo, or enjoying a meal on San Francisco's Fisherman's Wharf.

A trip to Terminal 21 is a journey around the world in nine floors. With its clean lines and elegant curves, the exterior of the building looks a lot like an airport and the signage inside follows suit, announcing the floors with signs that would be familiar to anyone who has spent time in an airport. Each level of the nine-floor, 600-store mall is themed on a different city, and iconic features from those cities have been cleverly woven into the design.

The main entrance level is Paris, complete with a replica of the Eiffel Tower, of course, and the Arc de Triomphe. The second floor is London, where an old red double-decker bus is parked between the shops, and a red telephone box and large post box add to the sense of British charm, while the toilets are cleverly modelled on an Underground station. Throughout Terminal 21 the toilets are a highlight of a visit to each floor – each one continuing the theme of the city, and each one unlike any other. Other destinations featured are the Caribbean, Rome, Istanbul, San Francisco (with an impressive replica of the Golden Gate Bridge that spans the void between floors four and five) and Hollywood which is, of course, the mall's cinema complex.

An unbeatable view of Bangkok

Terminal 21 was designed by P and T Group which, over its 150 years in existence, has created some of the most iconic buildings in South-East Asia. One of them is the beautiful 78-storey King Power Mahanakhon, which appears to spiral from the Bangkok skyline. From 2016 until 2018 it was Thailand's tallest building: the bar and 314-metre-high observation deck offer incredible views of Bangkok (kingpowermahanakhon.co.th).

SHRINE TO MAE NAK

⑬

Where a legendary female ghost is honoured

Wat Mahabut, 747/1 Soi On Nut 7, Suan Luang
Daily 7.30am–5pm

Mae Nak (Mother Nak) lived near Wat Mahabut about 150 years ago. According to one version of what has now become legend, Mae Nak was pregnant when her husband was conscripted as a soldier, and both she and her baby died while he was away. Mae Nak was so distraught about never seeing her husband again that she and her baby rose from the grave.

When her husband returned, the legend continues, neighbours wanted to warn him that the woman and baby, who appeared to be his family, were in fact ghosts. Not many were brave enough to tell him, however, as Mae Nak ensured that anyone who interfered with her family life died a gruesome death. One day, while cooking in their stilted house, Mae Nak absentmindedly reached an arm through the floorboards to pick up something she had dropped. Her husband ran screaming in terror and took shelter in a nearby temple. The infuriated Mae Nak and her baby wreaked havoc on the whole community until both of them were captured by an exorcist. The spirits were imprisoned in a jar that was thrown into the river, but when a fisherman netted the jar and opened it, he unwittingly inflicted a further diabolical chain of events on the neighbourhood. Finally, after more gruesome attacks, the spirits were captured by a powerful monk (see p. 224).

Much later, the villagers felt sorry for Mae Nak and her baby, so they built a shrine to them at Mahabut Temple. The shrine is popular with young women wishing for a good love-match and older women who are hoping to retain the affection of a straying husband. You will see women making offerings – jewellery, clothes, money for Mae Nak and toys for the baby – before whispering to the effigy of the ghost mother. Young men who are hoping to avoid army service come here too (Mae Nak's husband was a reluctant soldier, after all), but many say that it is a dangerous place for women who are pregnant or trying for a child.

The TV at the shrine is always on, since Mae Nak has become a big fan of Thai soap operas. It is not known, however, whether she saw any of the several films telling her story (see page 140) – including a 1959 classic, a 2012 3D version, a 2013 comedy-horror box-office hit, and even a children's animated movie called simply *Nak*.

Mae Nak is not the only female spirit in residence here: Nang Ta-khian (see p. 132) is said to reside in a tree by the main shrine.

BATCAT MUSEUM

The crown jewels of superhero memorabilia

3701 Srinagarindra Road, Bang Kapi
facebook.com/batcat.museum
Monday to Friday 10am–5pm; Saturday and Sunday 9am–8pm

The Batcat Museum houses a stunning exhi[bition] collectibles. Three rooms and two mezzanines h[ave] to accommodate truly gigantic fibreglass figures (some high) of The Hulk, Superman, Captain America, Spider[-man/] Woman and The Silver Surfer, and are filled with more t[han] models, games, magazines, books and costumes.

Needless to say, Batman is the true superhero among supe[r] in the Batcat collection and there is an entire room dedicat[ed to] him. There is even a life-size fibreglass replica of the Batmobile. [It's] fascinating to realise that a supposedly timeless character like Batma[n] has been through such a period of evolution – perhaps it was deemed that when he first appeared on colour TV the original bat-suit should be blue, since black might have suggested that he was a bad-guy. Real nerds will appreciate an opportunity to peruse the entire metamorphosis since the character first appeared (in 1939 in the May issue of *Detective Comics*, if you must know).

The museum is incredibly well laid out, with industrial-style high-level walkways, free-hanging doors (à la *Monsters Inc*) and Batcave-style low-lighting. Apart from the many oversized figures that will wow the children (and the villains like The Joker and Chucky the Doll that might freak them out), there are countless shelves stacked with thousands of enthralling miniatures dating back to the very beginnings of the superhero genre. Flat-screen TVs will thrill older visitors with nostalgic re-runs of 1960s Supermarionation (marionette puppets with electric moving parts) classics like *Thunderbirds*, *Joe 90* and *Stingray*.

Younger children will be thrilled by life-size figures of characters from *The Simpsons*, *Monsters Inc*, *Toy Story* and *Pokemon*, but only real comic buffs are likely to recognise more obscure figures like the Masked Rider, Captain Action, Ultraman and The Green Lantern. The latter must have confused the Thai public when he first appeared in DC Comics back in 1959, because in Bangkok a green lantern was the symbolic precursor to the red light which became such a notorious symbol of the city (see p. 91).

Superhero fans will also want to make a pilgrimage to Wat Pariwat (see p. 214) to see a temple with its own effigies of Batman, Captain America and Superman.

que collection to surpass all

Kritha, Bang Kapi
/ 3607
Sunday 10am–3pm
on by appointment only; entry is 500 baht per person

The Prasart Museum is an astounding celebration of Thai antï Beautiful buildings – each one a nod to Thai history – stan an enchanting expanse of gardens, ponds and shady walkways. buildings contain a good sample of the historic wealth of this countr there are priceless burial jars so ornate that they might have been usec at the burial of a king 2,000 years ago; gorgeous 600-year-old Khmer ceramics; and some of the world's finest pieces of Bencharong (see p. 215).

There is a Chinese Guanyin Shrine, several pavilions, and a beautiful teak *hŏr drai* (a stilted library in a lotus pond that offers protection from termites and fire). There is also a Khmer temple, shrouded by jungle vegetation that makes you feel like you have stumbled into *The Heart of Darkness*, and the Red Palace, which was built with rare golden teak and wooden dowels instead of nails.

Even the gardens boast a spectacular collection of antiques: 500-year-old glazed stoneware, ancient Buddha and Brahmin images, and an antique belfry saved from a ruined temple in Nonthaburi. The gardens are full of rare and unusual indigenous plants and trees, many of which were selected for their importance in Thai literature, tradition or herbal medicine.

The heart of the museum's collection is a European neo-colonial style house which has polished marble floors and Baroque ceilings, and is stacked with priceless artefacts, many of which belonged to kings and emperors. They are so precious that photography is prohibited and we are forbidden even to describe the objects that are on display there.

The museum, which opened in 1981, is the private collection of real estate tycoon Prasart Vongsakul, who took about a decade to prepare the 5-acre property. He still works as "head gardener" and strongly believes that the historic wealth of Thailand must be kept in the country. Khun Prasart began working when he was seven years old and has devoted his life to this collection: "I never married, and I never had children," he once told the *New York Times*. "What you see here are my children."

Look out for the daybed that belonged to Rama III, and for a carved Qing-dynasty screen that Khun Prasart, in leaner times, once fell in love with. He spent virtually all his savings (about US$675) on it at that time. It is now valued at about US$33,000.

South Bangkok

ARA SRI GURU
SABHA

reakfast with Bangkok's Sikh community

kkraphet Road, Phra Nakhon
24 hours
kfast served Monday to Saturday 8am–10am, Sunday 8am–1pm
ess code: modest. No short dresses or skirts; shoulders must be covered; men's hirts must be tucked in. All visitors must cover their heads with the saffron-coloured headcloths supplied.

The unassuming gateway to Gurudwara Sri Guru Singh Sabha is little wider than a parking space, yet it is the entrance to one of Bangkok's most unexpected secrets. The six-storey place of worship for the Sikh community offers an eye-opening cultural experience amid a truly heart-warming atmosphere of pure Eastern hospitality.

The first Sikhs to arrive in Bangkok were the textile dealers, in around 1890. They held prayers in family homes until 1912, when the growing community then rented a wooden house for use as a *gurudwara*, a place of worship and assembly for Sikhs. Within a year they had outgrown that building and so rented another one. In 1932 they bought the land on which Gurudwara Sri Guru Singh Sabha now stands.

During a bombing raid in World War II, several hundred Sikhs were sheltering in the temple when two 1,000-pound bombs crashed through the roof – miraculously both failed to explode and nobody died. Decades later the *gurudwara* was renovated and the one you see today, an enormous white building dominated by arches and domes, was completed in 1981 and is the focal point for a community of about 70,000 people.

The formidable building is respected by locals of other faiths who recognise it as one of the most hospitable temples in the city. Visitors are warmly welcomed and the temple staff – most of whom are volunteers performing *sewa* (the Sikh practice of rendering service) – will show you where to remove your shoes.

In the Darbar congregation hall you can attend a Sikh prayer meeting, which is particularly fascinating since TV screens around the walls provide Thai, English and Punjabi subtitles to the captivating *kirtan* ("scripture singing") performed by the temple musicians.

Every day in the Guru ka Langar (dining room) a free communal breakfast of vegetarian *thali* – often rice, lentil daal, Punjabi bread and vegetable curry – is served. *Langar* – best described as dining together from a common kitchen – symbolises selfless service, love and brotherhood, and the idea is that anyone is welcome, regardless of caste, creed, gender or social status (although men and women must sit on opposite sides of the room).

Despite the enforced silence, there is a wonderful atmosphere of friendship and conviviality and you will feel very welcome with smiles and nods from fellow diners.

The "bone-receiving hall" with an intriguing war history

Wat Ratchaburana, 133/18 Tri Phet Road, Phra Nakhon
Daily 7am–4pm

Wat Ratchaburana – often called by its old na[...] is the location of an intriguing Japanese *noko[...]* The building is a smaller replica of Kyoto's famous Kink[...] Pavilion, and although it is now forbidden to enter it, the oss[...] to house a 700-year-old Buddha statue brought here from Japa[...] the remains of an undetermined number of people.

The *nokotsudo* was built when Bangkok's Japanese comm[...] petitioned the king in 1932 for a place to store the "cremains" (as[...] and charred bones) of their dead. In 1943, during World War II, mos[...] of the temple complex was destroyed in an Allied bombing raid, but by a strange twist of fate, only the Japanese ossuary was left untouched.

This backdrop became the scene for one of the most bizarre dramas of World War II when a man that a British Intelligence operative labelled "one of the most dangerous men on the planet" went into hiding in the ossuary. Lieutenant Colonel Masanobu Tsuji was wanted for war crimes that included the massacre of Chinese during the Sook Ching purge in Singapore, the Bataan Death March in the Philippines, and even a macabre ritualistic act of cannibalism in Burma. It must have been a strange (although cunningly chosen) place to stay: the temple was largely flattened by bombing, and since the Wat Liab generating plant had also been put out of action by the bombs, two old Mitsubishi submarines were moored nearby in the Chao Phraya River to keep the electricity going and the trams running.

Tsuji faked suicide and is believed to have left his hideout in the ossuary at the end of October 1945 (two months after Japan surrendered). From there the man whom one contemporary nicknamed "The God of Evil" escaped to Japan, where today a monument to him stands in Kaga City. One conspiracy theory is that Tsuji was the hitman who murdered Rama VIII in 1946 (see p. 45), but most experts claim he had left Bangkok by then. In 1961 Tsuji finally disappeared in Laos. (A top-secret CIA dispatch from 1962 – declassified in 2005 – sugge[...] that he might have ended his days as an advisor to the North Vie[...]amese Army.)

Since the war, the ossuary has been tended by [...]sident Japanese monks, serving here on a three-year rotation.

...owest mansion in Bangkok

...rapha Phirom, Phra Nakhon

Close to the foot of Memorial Bridge (see p. 186) there is an elegant mansion with a clock tower central to its façade and large trees growing around the property's perimeter. At first glance you might assume it is "just" a regular European-style mansion, but take a look at the building from a slight angle and you will see that the entire structure is only 4 metres deep. It looks as though a façade had been neatly sliced off a mansion and transplanted on to the bank of the Chao Phraya River.

This building is, essentially, a nostalgic nod to Bangkok's postal system. When Thailand's very first post office opened in 1883 it was located inside a building called Praisaneeyakan, and the headquarters remained there until they were relocated in 1927. Praisaneeyakan was demolished in 1982 to make way for the Phra Pok Klao road and bridge, which were built to alleviate congestion on Memorial Bridge (and which, incidentally, brought an end to its functioning as a bascule bridge).

The façade of Praisaneeyakan was featured on a postage stamp the following year to commemorate the centenary of Thailand's postal system, and as people still associated that mansion with the Post Office, a replica of the façade was built close to its original site in 2004. At one stage there was a museum of sorts in the building, but it seems to be permanently closed now.

Thailand's postal service was established during the reign of Rama V (1868 to 1910), when the first stamps were issued for the delivery of the daily newspaper *Khow Ratchakarn*. The Solot Series is the name given to the country's first set of six stamps, which were made in England. The stamps showed the same portrait of Rama V and varied in colour according to the value of the stamp. Because the stamps in this series did not state that they were from Thailand or indicate their value, they were updated in 1887 to adhere to the Universal Postal Union regulations. These, as well as other Thai stamps, are on display at the Sam Sen Nai Philatelic Museum (2 Phahonyothin Road, Phaya Thai; open Friday to Sunday 8am- 5pm).

THE SECRETS
OF MEMORIAL BRIDGE

A "cousin" of the Sydney Harbour Bridge

Wang Burapha Phirom, Phra Nakhon
Note: Memorial Bridge is also known as Phra Phuttayotfa Bridge, Saphan Phut
Bridge, Phut Bridge and Buddha Bridge

Memorial Bridge opened on 6 April 1932 to commemorate 150 years of the reign of the Chakri Dynasty, the ruling royal house of Thailand. The beautiful steel structure was designed and built by Dorman Long – the same British company (still in operation today) that built the Sydney Harbour Bridge, which opened three weeks before Memorial Bridge.

The construction of Memorial Bridge, which took just over two years, was a mammoth undertaking. The land on either side of the river was notoriously marshy, the river itself 20 metres deep, and the flow of the current relatively strong. Reinforced concrete foundation posts were therefore built to 30 metres below the riverbed in order to carry the weight of the 1,430-tonne, 230-metre-long structure. When viewed from the river, the elegant shape of the bridge gives a clue to its functionality: for 50 years the two middle sections could be lifted, allowing taller ships to pass through. The bascule bridge was sealed forever in 1981, however, when construction was underway on the adjacent Phra Pok Klao Bridge.

The official opening of Memorial Bridge was a day wh[...]
with some trepidation by the people of Thailand. Since th[...]
Rama I there had been a legend that the founding king of th[...]
dynasty had prophesied his house would reign for 150 year[...]
opening of the bridge and the celebration of what is now know[...]
Chakri Day went smoothly, but less than three months later, an alm[...]
bloodless coup saw Thailand transition from an absolute monarchy to[...]
constitutional monarchy.

A layout that forms an arrow, the weapon of the Hindu god Rama

Take a look at the structure on Google Maps, and a shape becomes immediately apparent: the layout of the bridge forms the shape of an arrow. The ornamental gardens on the Thonburi side of the Chao Phraya River form the arrowhead, the bridge itself the shaft and the ornamental gardens (with a statue of Rama I created by Silpa Bhirasri, see p. 66) on the east of the river form the fletching.

The symbolism? An arrow is the weapon of the Hindu god Rama – and all kings in the Chakri dynasty are referred to as Rama. Incidentally, the emblem of the Chakri dynasty itself is a discus and a trident (the Chakra is a disc-like weapon used by the Hindu god Vishnu, and the Trisula is a principal symbol of Buddhism and Hinduism).

...k's "Little Lisbon"

...udichin Museum
...dsaban Road, Thonburi
...day to Sunday 9.30am–6pm

The Portuguese love-affair with Thailand extends back to 1511, but even so, stumbling across a Portuguese village on the west bank of the Chao Phraya River is likely to come as a something of a surprise.

Portuguese mercenaries had long proved useful to the Siamese kings, and in 1770 the Portuguese community was granted permission to build a Catholic church on the riverbank in Thonburi – 250 years later, the Church of Santa Cruz remains the centre of this unlikely "Little Lisbon" quarter. The renovation of the church in the 19th century was heavily influenced by Chinese touches, resulting in the "Kudichin" nickname (Chinese Church) by which Santa Cruz and the surrounding community is commonly known today.

A sedate saunter through the tangle of alleyways that stretches along the riverbank here reveals a very unexpected side of Bangkok. Baan Kudichin Museum, which opened in an old family home in 2016, is the ideal starting point since it offers a wonderful insight into this unexpected Thai-Portuguese community. The family-run museum boasts three storeys of intriguing exhibits, with displays on the history, arts, tradition and cuisine of the descendants of the Portuguese settlers.

The museum's café is a great place to grab lunch, and even a cursory glance down the menu – *fios de ovos, queijadas de Coimbra, pastel de nata* – highlights the fact that Portuguese culture remains vibrant here.

Wander around the Kudichin neighbourhood (often spelled Kudeejeen, Kudi Chin, Kudi Cheen or even Kudi Jeen) and you will find other Thai-Portuguese fusion specialities, such as Kudichin cake and *e-pae* biscuits, which are smoked in a jar with a scented candle. Any doubts that these remain staunchly family businesses are allayed by the names of some of the establishments here: Auntie Lek's Shop, Auntie Amphan's Shop and Grandma Pao's Niece's Shop.

One of the most evocative of Kudichin's many Portuguese-style bakeries is to be found in a lane just past the museum. Just ask for Thanusingha and you will find yourself sitting in the front room of an old timber townhouse enjoying the fruits of several generations of baking talent. Be sure to try *khanom farang Kuti Chin* ("foreign snack from Kudichin"), a crumbly pastry with raisins, topped with sugar and candied melon.

A fairy-tale mountain surrounded by miniature "houses"

Wat Prayurawongsawat Worawihan (Wat Prayoon), 24 Prajadhipok Road, Thonburi
Daily 9am– 6pm

Until the reign of Rama VII (1925 to 1935) n. (*khao mor*) were popular in Bangkok. People . *khao mor* since the Ayutthaya Era, and in flat Bangko. became an important decorative feature in temples and r There are some beautiful examples of *khao mor* around the Wat Pho, but perhaps the most impressive is to be seen at Wat .

The *khao mor* at Wat Prayoon rises from a moat-like pond, a. "mountain" is shrouded by trees and bushes that shade the struct built onto the carefully created ledges and layers of stone. This miniatu. mountain was built during the reign of Rama III (1824 to 1851), and one legend has it that the inspiration came when the king, reading by candlelight, noticed that the molten wax had formed into an attractive little peak. He admired it in the presence of one of his advisers, Somdej Chao Phraya Maha Prayurawong, who ordered that a replica mountain be built on a coffee plantation he owned in Thonburi.

The *khao mor* must have caused quite a stir when it loomed on the horizon in 1828, because very soon noble families were commissioning miniature pavilions, stupas and pagodas to decorate the mountain. There is even a little concrete crematorium and a small cave housing a miniature reclining Buddha. The "houses", which are actually miniature mausoleums, were apparently commissioned at enormous prices that approached the cost of *real* houses.

Although Wat Prayoon was built during the reign of Rama III, its significance as a religious site dates back much further. During two whirlwind days of excavation here in 2007, almost 2,000 Buddhist statues and amulets, some as old as 800 years, were found in two crypts. Some of the finest are in display in the temple's Prayoon Bhandakharn Museum, along with what is said to be a piece of the Buddha's bone.

The 60-metre-high Lanka-style chedi at the temple houses another relic of the Buddha. You are welcome to climb barefoot into the hollow shrine inside the chedi, but once inside you will see that the exit is formed by an extremely low tunnel that you must crawl through. A temple guide explains that this causes you to "maintain consciousness" that you are in a sacred place.

...l sanctuary in the heart of Bangkok

...ra Sri Nagarindra (Princess Mother Memorial Park), Soi Somdech
...raya 3, Khlong Sarn
...Daily 6am–6pm
...eum: Daily (except public holidays) 8.30am–4.30pm

Affectionately known as Suan Somdet Ya, the small b[ ]
serene Princess Mother Memorial Park was built to [ ]
memory of Her Royal Highness Princess Srinagarindra (1900– [ ]
Princess Mother. The quiet enclave of towering trees and broa[ ]
tropical plants creates a delightful sanctuary that, surprisingly, is n[ ]
even on weekends, despite its close proximity to central Bangkok.

At the park entrance there is a bronze statue of the Princess Moth[ ]
seated casually on a bench – an endearing image of a compassionat[ ]
woman who was very much loved by the Thai people. The Princess
Mother was a nurse by training, and she set up many public health, social
welfare and education initiatives – beneath the bronze bench there is soil
from every part of Thailand she visited in order to provide relief, aid or to
connect with the people.

The Princess Mother, whose birth name was Sangwan Chukramol, was
born and raised in the Klong Sarn neighbourhood adjacent to the park –
that is why her son, Rama IX, established the park here. His intention
was to commemorate his mother's 96th birthday (an auspicious birthday
as it marks a person's eighth 12-year cycle – see p. 53) by preserving her
childhood home, but she passed away before the park was completed.

Within the park there is a building similar to the Princess Mother's
childhood home. There are also two museum rooms that contain
memorabilia from her life, including porcelain pieces she painted and
ceramics she sculpted, a few Buddha images she carved, her badminton
racquet, and skis (skiing was the Princess Mother's favourite sport as she
had lived for many years in Switzerland). The museum and park are well
signed with lots of information (in English) that gives wonderful insights
into the life and character of the Princess Mother.

The mother of kings

The Princess Mother was among the first generation of Thai girls to
receive an education (see p. 55). In 1917 she was awarded a scholarship
to study nursing in the USA, where she met Prince Mahidol Adulyadej.
The prince, the 69th child of Rama V, studied medicine and went on
to be heralded as Thailand's Father of Modern Medicine and Public
Health. They had a daughter and two sons, both of whom became
kings (Rama VIII and Rama IX).

Lhong 1919 is the beautifully preserved hea
Cihong, a 19th-century Mandarin mogul who ᴠ
as a rice trader. The two-hectare compound, which is
fifth-generation descendants of Chen Cihong, gives visito
to explore the Sino-Siamese port where thousands of immigr
have first set foot on Siamese soil.

Huo Chuan Lhong (meaning "steamship terminal") opened ᴨ
1850. The complex was constructed as three buildings surroundɩ
courtyard, following feng shui principles where the courtyard allows ꜰ
connection between heaven and earth. In pride of place facing the river
is the lovingly maintained shrine to the sea goddess Mazu – known
as Chao Mae Thabthim in Thai (see p. 246) – which is still in almost
constant use by worshippers. The three statues in the shrine, brought here
from China over a century ago, represent Mazu during the three stages
of her manifestation: as the young girl who could predict the weather
and save mariners and fishermen; as the goddess and benefactress; and
as the Queen of Heaven.

Apart from Mazu Court there are two other courtyards: Sang Xing
Court and Yinyang Court. The buildings along both sides of Mazu Court
and into Sang Xing Court once held offices and *gudang* warehouses
("go-downs"), but today they boast a lovely café, three restaurants,
several arts, crafts and even antique outlets and a spa. The buildings
are built of teak and brick, and are decorated with plaster window
borders and doorframes, many of which still feature the original murals
depicting traditional Chinese life. Many of these have been restored
but the few which remain in a crumbling state of near dilapidation
(some protected by glass) only serve to make the architecture feel more
appealingly authentic.

Lhong 1919 would be worth a visit for the evocative little café
alone. Set in a building which is over 150 years old, Plearnwan Panich
(Merchants' Pier) has been very sensitively renovated to look like an old-
style Chinese teahouse. It features local culinary specialities including
luk khrueng ("half-breed" coffee), which combines old-style Thai
coffee brewing with international coffee beans, and toast smothered in
condensed milk and *kaya*, a sort of coconut custard that was created as
a substitute for fruit jam during Malaysia's colonial era.

ɹan of Bangkok

ao Phraya Road,

Close to the glitzy Icon Siam mall, the broa
fort stand rooted to the banks of the Chao Phr.
built to protect an expanding Bangkok, is now hidden
cluster of harbour-department housing.

For the position of Fort Pong Patchamit to make sense,
step back to the days before Bangkok existed. When Taksin
(see p. 16) moved the Siamese capital from Ayutthaya to Thont
set about establishing a strategic network of *khlongs* (canals) that Ra
then expanded when, 15 years later, he moved the capital over to t
east bank of the Chao Phraya River (see p. 20). Both kings had wanted
to replicate the geo-political template of Ayutthaya, a city enclosed
by two rivers and with a sophisticated system of canals and moats to
protect, drain and support the ancient city.

By the time Rama IV came to power, Bangkok was in dire need
of additional space, so in 1852 the king built Khlong Phadung Krung
Kasem ("Canal Upholding the City's Happiness") as a third line of
defence – thus doubling the size of the city. He then built seven forts
along the 5.5-km-long canal, and to guard Bangkok from invaders from
the sea, Fort Pong Patchamit was established on the western bank of
the river.

Three years after the forts were built the Bowring Treaty was signed
(see p. 72), and the riverbank around Fort Pong Patchamit started to
crowd with trading vessels (see p. 194). From Fort Pong Patchamit and
Fort Pit Patchaneuk (which no longer exists) on the opposite bank, gun
salutes were fired to welcome royal envoys, and a signal flagpole (which
still stands today) was erected at Fort Pong Patchamit to identify the
owners of vessels arriving or leaving the harbour.

The original course of the Chao Phraya River

Almost 500 years ago the course of the meandering Chao Phraya River
was altered for the first time to shorten the distance from the Gulf
of Siam to Ayutthaya. Part of the river's man-made section – once
called Lat Bangkok – flanks one of Bangkok's most popular tourist
destinations: Rattanakosin Island. Khlong Bangkok Noi, the canal at
the Siriraj Bimuksthan Museum (see p. 124), and Khlong Bangkok
Yai are both the original course of the river. The diversion, created in
1542, shortened the river by 14 km.

...sweetest music is made

There is an old Thai saying that goes "if the dan~~ce~~ flute", but nobody would ever blame the flutes ~~of~~ little neighbourhood at the edge of Thonburi, where p~~eople~~ playing flutes for more than two centuries, has a reputatio~~n~~ some of the most beautiful sounds in Thailand.

Bang Sai Kai quarter is known simply as Baan Lao after th~~e~~ community that settled here about 230 years ago. The musical ma~~...~~ the *khlui* (flute) and *kaan* (bamboo organ) became victims of their success: Rama IV, fearing for the future of traditional Thai music as ~~...~~ people turned to the attractive Laotian tunes, outlawed the musicians o~~f~~ Baan Lao sometime around 1860. So, ever innovative, they tuned their talents towards producing fine instruments for Thai musicians to play.

There is still a handful of family-run workshops in the tangled alleys of Baan Lao: wander down Soi Itsaraphap 15 and you will see hand-painted signs leading to the last few flute-producing homes in this traditional neighbourhood -- and you will be welcome to visit if they are open.

"The best flutes are made from monastery bamboo, which we call *ruak*," explains Sunai Kinbuppaa (known to his friends as P'Chang – Big Brother Elephant), a fifth-generation master flute-maker in Baan Lao. Monastery bamboo (*Thyrsostachys siamensis*) is now rare, so the flute-makers are turning to hardwoods such as Asian rosewood (*Dalbergia odorifera*). Impurities in the wood were traditionally disguised by dripping molten lead onto the wood to form beautiful lacework patterns, and in the old days it was believed that music from the finest flutes had the power to cure illness and ease the spirits of the dead. Particularly prized hardwood flutes are still made from a type of black wood that is said to house a deity called Nang Ta-khian (see p. 132) -- these flutes must be made with particular care and can reach prices in excess of 10,000 baht.

The beautiful bamboo flutes (which sell for between about 2,000 and 8,000 baht) are still polished with brick-dust and coconut fibre, producing a sheen that is impossible to replicate with sandpaper. The hole in the centre is filled with bees' wax before a heated rod is pushed through to even out the tiniest irregularities.

Bangkok's fleet of incredible temples

ng Rd, Sathon
.30pm

Bangkok is a city of remarkable temples and Wat Yanna
banks of the Chao Phraya River, is certainly one of its mos
ones. Here, in the centre of the temple complex, stands a 45-me
replica of an old trading junk. This ship-shaped building – wit.
chedis containing relics of the Buddha, representing the masts – is
temple's *viharn* (sermon hall), and it has been an integral part of V
Yannawa since its construction during the reign of Rama III (1824 t.
1851).

The Wat Yannawa complex was once the stable for a herd of holy
water buffalo, but they might have already disappeared when Rama III
made the forward-thinking decision to build the junk replica here. The
king, years before, had been his father's minister for commerce, and
had overseen the trading voyages of around 700 royal junks – during
the reign of Rama II (1809 to 1824), Bangkok was a significant centre
for junk building, and the trade generated enormous revenue for Siam.
In creating this junk replica, Rama III wanted to acknowledge and
honour the significant role the boats had played in the development of
his country.

The junk at Wat Yannawa is painted white – this is because during
the 19th century the origin of a junk was shown by the colour of its hull:
red junks were of Chinese origin, primarily from Northern Guangdong
Province, whereas white junks were Siamese. If you look closely, you will
notice that this junk replica is decorated with rather quizzical-looking
eyes on the bows – as if it were utterly bemused to find itself stranded
100 metres away from the river. Historically many sailors in this part
of the world believed that it was primarily these all-seeing eyes on the
bows of their vessels that prevented mishaps. Even today you will see
eyes painted on vessels of all sizes from Vietnam, through Hong Kong
and into coastal China, but this form of spiritual insurance has become
increasingly rare in Thailand.

Access into the temple's junk is through a door under its beam, but
this is for worshippers only. You can, however, walk around the junk
and its tended garden. If you walk right through the temple complex to
the river bank, you will also find a fish-feeding station where you can
make merit (see p. 19) – or just make a wish -- when you feed wild Chao
Phraya catfish.

TAKRAW AT TEOCHEW CEMETERY

(12)

Thrilling sport in a Chinese cemetery

12 Chan Road, Thung Wat Don, Sathon
Daily 4am–9pm; takraw is normally played around 5pm–7pm

akraw is surely one of the world's most exciti...
can watch a particularly dramatic version of t...
Cemetery, an unexpected location for an enchanting...

Technically, *takraw* is not a ball game at all but ...
woven basket traditionally made of wicker, but these da...
made from more durable plastic. A rare version of the gam...
"hoop *takraw*", is played most evenings in Teochew Cemet...
net (something like an oversized lobster trap) that is suspend...
5 metres above the centre of the court. The objective is for the cr...
players to compete to punt the ball into the net with the foot, k...
elbow or forehead. The net is then lowered to retrieve the ball and t...
game starts again. The game is made still more spectacular with the
inclusion of trick kicks purely for fun, and the players at Teochew are
invariably as friendly as they are talented – you will be welcome to watch
and photograph ... or even invited to have a go.

In other parks around Bangkok *takraw* is often played as an
impromptu kickabout with a group of players trying simply to keep the
ball off the ground while performing tricks in the form of scissor-kicks
and unexpected punts with the back of the elbow (perhaps unique in
the world of ball-sports). A more competitive version of the game – also
played at Teochew Cemetery – features teams of two or three players
on courts with a badminton net. The most dramatic manoeuvre in this
version is a slam-kick – a 360-degree-back-flip-bicycle-spin-kick – that
players execute almost entirely upside down ... frequently landing on
the back of their neck.

When the weather is dry you can expect to see *takraw* at Teochew
Cemetery (see p. 206) on most afternoons around 5pm, but you
might come across the more regular versions of the game in many
parks around Bangkok, including Benjasiri and Lumphini parks.

The game is found throughout South-East Asia and is usually called
sepak takraw: *sepak* is Malay for "kick" while *takraw* is the Thai name
for the wicker ball. In Wat Mahanaparam, offerings of *takraw* balls are
made to Buddha, and at Wat Phra Keo, look out for a mural depicting
a monkey (some say it is the god Hanuman) executing a particularly
nimble back-heel-overhead-punt during a game of *takraw*.

͟est cemetery

Park, Soi Wat Prok, Sathon

Around 5,000 graves are crammed into Teochew Cemetery, which stretches over half a kilometre back from the ornate Chinese gateway on Soi Wat Prok. It is here that around dawn each morning, hundreds of fitness fanatics converge on what might well be the healthiest cemetery you will ever come across.

Residents of the neighbouring quarters come here to run, cycle, practise tai chi and aerobics, or to play badminton or basketball. There is even a kickboxing training area and a gym with more than 100 exercise machines. There are also a couple of appealing little cafés for those who prefer to sit quietly in the sun and watch other people working out.

What makes this park unusual is that, in Chinese culture, people are traditionally very reticent about associating themselves with anything concerning death. Few Bangkokians from other areas are even aware of the existence of this cemetery park, and many would be shocked to hear that such a thing even exists.

However, Teochew Cemetery has become a place where living residents (the majority in this area are of Chinese descent) associate cheerfully and unreservedly among their deceased family members. You might find occasional spine-tingling references to this "haunted park" in blogs and the cemetery listed on the odd off-beat Bangkok tour itinerary. The earliest graves are well over a hundred years old, and some claim that the park is haunted by immigrant Chinese from the Teochew clan whose spirits were unable to return to their homeland.

Far from being a morbid place, however, there is something refreshingly cheerful about the bustling, packed pathways and running tracks that weave among the clusters of well-tended horseshoe-shaped graves that are sometimes said to be representative of the womb. The few visitors who take time to soak up the atmosphere here discover that far from being gloomy, Teochew Cemetery Park is surely one of Bangkok's most charming parks.

In the evening, between about 5pm and 7pm, this is one of the best places in the city to watch the spectacular sport of *takraw* (see p. 204) and there is even a karaoke spot for those who want to take "whistling past the graveyard" to more literal extremes.

PE RUCK CANAL

Bangkok's most haunted waterway

33 Soi Phetchahung, Bang Krachao

While there are communities scattered all over Bang Krachao – the island often referred to as Bangkok's green lung – nobody has ever lived along Pe Ruck canal. According to the residents of Bang Krachao, the little forest-lined canal called Khlong Pe Ruck is the most haunted spot in Bangkok: here, they say, there are many Phi Tai Hong.

Malevolent spirits of all sorts, whether ghouls, ghosts, vampires or banshees, are referred to in Thai as *phi* (sometimes written as *pe*), and Phi Tai Hong is the Thai name for the vengeful ghost of any person who died an untimely death, and therefore harbours a dangerous hatred towards the living. It is a thing to be feared and avoided at all costs. You are unlikely to see many people strolling along Pe Ruck Canal, because as inhabitants of the area will tell you, many bodies have been found in this wild little section of forest-lined canal. "A weird twist of currents ensures that any drowned body will sooner or later end up being drawn into the eddies of Khlong Pe Ruck," they explain.

Even if it were not for such spirits, a simple walk down a forest pathway like this could be fraught with an astounding array of otherworldly dangers: a snake slithering across the track could be a sign that Phi Ngu (the ghost snake) is near, or the screech of an owl might herald the arrival of Phi Ka, a ghost that turns its victims into cannibals with an insatiable hunger for human livers.

On the approach to the canal you will pass through coconut plantations (a favoured haunt of Phi Maphrao, the coconut ghost) and stands of wild bananas that are said to be the lair of Nang Tani, who you will recognise by her green dress and blood-red lips, and the fact that she hovers a few feet above the ground. Few villagers will allow the wild bananas to grow close to their house, and even in the forest, you will sometimes see these trees decorated with offerings to propitiate Nang Tani. The ghosts of Mae Nak (see p. 172) and Nang Ta-khian (see p. 132) have both been elevated to the level of minor goddesses.

While outsiders might view these apparitions as quaint folktales, they are a very real part of Thai life and culturally sensitive travellers should show respect by keeping any scepticism to themselves.

SRI NAKHON KHUEAN KHAN PARK AND BOTANICAL GARDEN

⑮

A charming green lung in the heart of "Pig Stomach Island"

73 Soi Wat Rat Rangsan, Bang Krachao
Daily, 5am–7pm

Signs all over Sri Nakhon Khuean Khan Park and Botanical Garden declare it "the best urban oasis of Asia". While this might be an

exaggeration, it is almost certainly the best place in Bangkok to take a breather from the frantic bustle of the city centre.

The Sri Nakhon Khuean Khan Park and Botanical Garden is tucked away in Bang Krachao, a 15-square-kilometre "island" that has the sort of relaxed rural appeal few people would expect to find in a city of almost 10 million inhabitants. The park is surrounded by Bangkok's "green lung" – an arc of hamlets, fields, forests and lakes that cover an area larger than the entire historical centre of old Bangkok.

The park itself is well maintained and there are wonderful cycling trails, pretty hump-back bridges and plenty of signs that provide interesting information on the area and its vegetation. More than just a place to relax, the botanical garden is often described as a "recreational area for eco-learning": the signboards shine a light onto such dimly understood mysteries as the communal life of the *shan rong* (stingless bee), how to harvest the fruit of the "suicide tree", and the "secrets of the nipa palm".

There is also a 7-metre-high birdwatching tower from where you might spot such rarities as Indian rollers, greater coucals or coppersmith barbets. In fact, between 60 and 100 bird species have been spotted in Sri Nakhon Khuean Khan Park (depending on which sign you choose to believe). The park is open until 7pm, and if you are still trying to spot white-throated kingfishers when the light begins to fade, look out for the floating specks of light as fireflies flit like fairies through the mangrove forests.

The city's most idyllic breathing space

Bang Krachao is sometimes referred to as Pig Stomach Island because of its shape: it juts into a bend of the Chao Phraya River and is "disconnected" by a canal. The island is the city's most idyllic breathing space and is well worth exploring over an entire day. Rent a bicycle (about 70 baht per day, from many points on the island) and consider bringing a picnic – while there are a few simple eateries and cafés, there are not many shops in Bang Krachao.

GANESHA STATUE AT MAHA DEVALAYA HINDU TEMPLE

A giant statue of the elephant god

Soi Wat Rat Rangsan, Bang Krachao
Daily 8am–8pm

The gigantic statue of the elephant-headed god Ganesha at Maha Devalaya Hindu Temple might be the most unexpected sight you will come across on Bang Krachao Island. It is about 6 metres tall, and even the rather cute rat that stares adoringly up from the god's feet is almost 1.5 metres tall.

In Thailand Ganesha is worshipped as the god of fortune and the remover of obstacles. As such, he is a great favourite with businesspeople and entrepreneurs, and some say that when business is down things can be improved by temporarily hanging his picture upside-down by way of punishment. Ganesha is also the god of the arts (even featuring in the emblem of the Thai Department of Fine Arts). Artists come to this statue to make offerings, and few Thai TV companies or film directors would begin shooting without first making an offering – perhaps marigold garlands, milk, sugarcane, traditional desserts or fruit – to the elephant-god.

The tree that forecasts lottery results

Step through the narrow gateway to the left of main shrine and you will find a much smaller, but equally fascinating, altar erected against the trunk of an old tree. It is said that this is the abode of Nang Ta-khian (see p. 132). You will notice brightly coloured dresses that her worshippers have donated in the hope that in return she will use the bark of this ancient tree as a screen to clue her devotees in on winning lottery numbers. Her worshippers here sprinkle powder on the tree-trunk (simple baby talc is, apparently, perfect) and try to decipher any numbers that appear in the white dust. Other examples of this lottery-forecasting lumber are to be found at Wat Mahabut (see p. 172) and Wat Prasat (see p. 132).

Legend has it that Shiva (the destroyer) accidentally beheaded his own son in a case of mistaken jealousy when – after an exceptionally long absence – he returned home to find his wife living with a young man. Once he realised that his victim was his own son, Shiva vowed to replace the head with that of whatever creature he first came across ... and the first animal he encountered was a young elephant. There are many versions of the story, but defenders of this one cite as evidence the fact that images of Ganesha usually portray him with a shattered right tusk, where Shiva's sword struck.

WAT PARIWAT

A temple with effigies of Donald Duck and David Beckham

734 Rama III Road, Yan Nawa
Daily 9am–5pm

On the altar in the ordination hall at Wat Pariwat there is a statue of David Beckham. It is said that in 1998 the abbot replaced a statue of a Garuda (the eagle-human bird in Buddhist and Hindu mythology) with his football hero. The effigy, in Manchester United strip, crouches next to a bizarre mural that depicts scenes from hell: starving figures are boiled alive while other naked "sinners" are pursued, bleeding, up cactus trees by slavering dogs.

It is a strange sight, but 100 metres from the ordination hall there is a compound that is even more surreal. A new temple has been decorated with an eclectic cast of stars including Donald Duck, Popeye, Batman (see p. 174), Captain America, Superman, Captain Hook, Wolverine and Che Guevara. You might recognise the yellow Pikachu Pokemon rabbit, the manga character Monkey D. Luffy, Dobby the slave (from *Harry Potter*) and a person – said to be Barack Obama – taking a selfie.

The inside of the temple is just as spectacular. In fact, everywhere you look there is something enthralling, and the high-relief sculptures are intricately designed. On one outer wall there is a whole workforce of what seem to be punk liberators (including a Mohican wielding a blowtorch, and a skinhead with a chainsaw) releasing a chained giant. The most beautiful pieces might be the very regal and realistic "animal gods" – a human-sized shark god, a monitor lizard god, and a lion god – all surrounded by their "animal disciples".

Two particularly bemusing questions which are provoked by this star-studded cast are: why is Pinocchio wearing a skirt, and why is Mickey Mouse revealing a pair of large breasts? These questions have never been answered by the artist Surin Phanumas, who spent 10 years sculpting the plaster figures and decorating them with shards of Bencharong porcelain. The renovation, which the abbot claims helps to attract younger worshippers, is estimated to have cost almost US$10 million.

Bencharong: beautiful shards of colour

Although *bencharong* translates as "five-coloured", Bencharong porcelain is usually decorated with between three and eight colours, and the style is characterised by repetitive geometric or floral designs. Its roots are in China, and the enamelled porcelain became popular in Siamese royal courts during the Ayutthaya Era. These days it is a popular souvenir from Thailand.

North Bangkok

PHAYA THAI PALACE

The city's most unusual royal residence

315 Ratchawithi Road, Ratchathewi
Tuesday and Thursday 1pm–3pm; Saturday and Sunday 9.30am–11.30am and
1.30pm–3.30pm

Phaya Thai is the most unusual palace in Bangkok. What makes it so intriguing – and unexpected – is that the palace looks like something out of a European fairy tale. With a distinctive spire and frescoed ceilings, delicate fretwork, French doors and tiered roofs, the building is a beautiful combination of Romanesque and neo-Gothic architecture. Grand staircases and open corridors abound.

The palace, which is now a military residence and hospital, was built by Rama V, who bought land along the banks of the Samsen canal in what was then a farming area. He "built a conglomeration of comfortable wooden buildings which he called Phaya Thai (Lord Thai) Palace, where he intended to retire with Queen Saowabha as a farmer after his abdication", wrote Prince Chula Chakrabongse in *Lords of Life* (River Books, 2019), which chronicles the kings of Thailand. The retreat was completed in 1909, and Rama V died only a few months later.

Queen Saowabha loved the property and lived there until she passed away almost a decade later. Rama VI then had all the buildings save one

dismantled to make way for a new royal residence. The original building that remains, called Phra Thinang Thewarat, is beautiful – its wooden walls are painted in shades of green and French doors line its sides.

The iconic part of the new building, the "turret" of the palace, is the Phiman Chakri Hall. It was built in 1920, and from the very top of the spire the Thai royal standard – yellow with a red garuda – was flown while Rama VI was in residence.

Queen of the night

During his reign Rama V rarely went to bed before 3am, and Queen Saowabha (see p. 52 and p. 55) adapted to his habits. After he died the queen lived an increasingly nocturnal life and it is said that in order for her to sleep peacefully during the day, traffic around Phaya Thai Palace was rerouted and birds were kept away by noiseless blowpipes. In the book *Lords of Life* Prince Chula Chakrabongse, a grandson of Queen Saowabha, recalls late-night visits with his grandmother, who had an unusual passion for cars (see p. 58). He outlines the schedule of her nights: Queen Saowabha would take breakfast at 10.30pm, receive visitors after 11pm, and have lunch or dinner at 2.30am. "The last of her visitors left at 5am, shortly after the queen herself went to sleep," he wrote.

ANTI-CORRUPTION MUSEUM ②

Thailand's honest exposé of corruption

165/1 Phitsanulok Road, Dusit
Monday to Friday 9am–4pm

The museum of the National Anti-Corruption Commission (NACC) should be a compulsory visit for anyone wishing to do business in Thailand, and even for the general public it makes for a surprisingly enthralling and entertaining visit. The museum's designers have succeeded in illustrating a potentially heavy subject with vibrant interactive exhibits.

Corruption is present in politics and business in many parts of the world, but there cannot be many countries that would choose to highlight it in such an honest way. It is well worth an hour or so of your time to take a stroll through the eight rooms dedicated to the exposure of corruption at all levels, from humble village leaders to prime ministers. Along the way you will learn that there is a whole glossary of slang related to different types of bribes: bribe offers are known as *tid sin bon*; bribe demands are *riak sin bon*; and a regularly paid bribe is referred to as *suay* (which could be translated as a "sweetener").

This excellent museum goes beyond the mere theories of corruption by highlighting some intriguing real-life cases. There are no punches pulled here and you will even read about the 1995 corruption scandal in which ex-Prime Minister Thaksin Shinawatra was implicated. This is not just a Thai problem, of course, and one very colourfully presented exhibit (featuring a life-size cut-out of a fire engine) highlights a 2008 case when the Austrian unit of the American defence contractor General Dynamics was tried for corruption relating to the US$183-million sale of 315 fire engines and 30 firefighting boats. According to a report in the *New York Times*, a former chief firefighter and a former deputy interior minister fled the country, and Steyr-Daimler-Puch Spezialfahrzeug (the Austrian unit) conveniently closed its Bangkok office before the

case even came to trial. The hundreds of abandoned fire engines are apparently still rusting in a parking lot in Bangkok's Sai Noi suburb.

While the museum is clearly aimed at encouraging Thai people (especially through the regular school-trips) to recognise and expose corruption, the majority of the displays are bilingual. Regardless of what country you come from, there are some very thought-provoking ideas that we can all benefit from.

WAT INTHARAWIHAN

The "unknown" temple with a 32-metre-tall Buddha

Wat Intharawihan, 144 Wisut Kasat Road, Phra Nakhon
Daily 6am–6pm

At Wat Intharawihan – colloquially called Temple of the Standing Buddha – there is an enormous gilded Buddha statue that stands 32 metres tall and more than 10 metres wide. It is an astounding sight and yet, despite being just a kilometre from the tourist-packed Khao San Road, few foreign visitors ever feast their eyes on this spectacle.

There are some who say that this Buddha's expression of amused patience developed over the 60 years it took to complete his construction. Work started on the statue (which is made of brick and stucco) during the last year of Rama IV's reign in 1867, continued right through the reigns of Rama V and Rama VI, and was finally completed in 1927, just five years before the revolution that brought about the end of absolute monarchy in Thailand. This statue's topknot and forehead contain relics of the Buddha which were donated by the government of Sri Lanka in 1978. Then a few years later, when Bangkok celebrated its bicentennial anniversary, the entire statue was covered with gilded Italian mosaic tiles.

The abbot responsible for its construction was Somdej Toh, who remains one of the most famous monks in Thai history. He is believed to have had magical powers, and some say it was he who finally restrained the rampaging spirit of Mae Nak and her ghost baby (see p. 172). The abbot died at the foot of his – still far from finished – Buddha in 1872.

Each day at Wat Pho, endless crowds parade past the 46-metre-long Reclining Buddha, and at Wat Phra Kaew the rather more diminutive but equally spectacular Emerald Buddha (which is 66 cm tall, made of jade and clothed in gold) draws busloads of sightseers. Few tourists make it to the peaceful Wat Intharawihan temple, however, and there is little information to be found. According to a sign in English in the street outside the temple, "some Thais believe that the bigger the image the more merit power it contains". If this is true, then there must be almost immeasurable merit in such an awe-inspiring monument. (For more on merit-making see p. 19.)

CERAMIC TOKENS AT THE BANK ④
OF THAILAND MUSEUM

The gambling chips that were used as currency

Bank of Thailand Learning Centre
273 Samsen Road, Phra Nakhon
NOTE: Many online sources say that the museum is at Bang Khun Phrom
Palace – this is its old location.
Tuesday to Sunday 9.30am–8pm

Acollection of gambling chips is an unlikely display at a bank, but the Bank of Thailand Museum holds an intriguing array of the ceramic tokens that became an integral, yet unofficial, part of Bangkok's economy.

Ceramic and sometimes glass chips, called *pi kra bueng* (some sources simply call them *pi*) were imported from China and used as tokens in gambling houses across Bangkok. Sources say there were between 5,000 and 7,000 designs of various shapes and sizes, with images and symbols stamped on them to indicate the gambling house's name, a poetic phrase, an auspicious character or a blessing. They are lovely to look at, but why did these tokens end up here?

By the 1860s, Thai coins were minted from silver, tin or copper. In 1873, however, the price of the metals increased sharply, and astute entrepreneurs smelted the tin and copper coins to export the metals. With a severe shortage of small-denomination coins, people who lived around the gambling houses began to use *pi* to buy low-value goods, and for two years, until Rama IV banned it, *pi* was commonly used as currency around Bangkok.

The Bank of Thailand Museum, on the banks of the Chao Phraya River, is a building of striking geometric design that opened in 1969 as the country's first note-printing works (before that, bank notes were printed in Europe). The museum has well-documented (in Thai, English and Braille) exhibitions of the printing work's first machines, and the development of money and the economy in Thailand. It is surprisingly interesting, even for those who are not finance-minded. Be sure to pop into the library and the café for spectacular views of the Rama VIII bridge.

Thailand's first bank

Thailand's first bank was established in 1904 as "The Book Club". It was an experiment by Prince Mahaisara Ratchaharuthai (a brother of Rama V) who, to keep it under the radar, ensured the bank's shophouse office displayed books that could be read there or borrowed. Within four years the bank was declared a success – it was renamed Siam Commercial Bank and moved into its purpose-built premises on the banks of the Chao Phraya River. The bank still operates from there today. With its turn-of-last-century banking hall, the grand old building is worth a look if you are in the Talat Noi area – it is next to the Holy Rosary Church.

GOLDEN TEAK MUSEUM

A building made of teak that is almost 500 years old

90 Sri Ayutthaya Road, Dusit
Daily 9am–5pm

Stepping into this great timber building is like walking into the heart of a polished-wood forest. The foundations for the Golden Teak Museum building are formed by 59 vast teak trunks – each one is far too large to reach around, but if ever there was a building that deserved a hug, this is it.

This princely mansion was built entirely out of teak, the queen of timbers. The Research and Training Centre of Tree Ring and Climate

Change at Mahidol University conducted a study to determine the age of the pillars, and researchers took samples from 15 of the main teak supports for "dendrochronological analysis" (i.e. counting growth rings) and radiocarbon dating. They concluded that the timber used in the construction was around 479 years old.

Originally constructed in Phrae Province, Northern Thailand, as a private home, this majestic two-storey teak dwelling (measuring over 1,000 square metres in total) was up for sale in 1988. It was destined to be chain-sawed into sellable pieces for its valuable timber but, fortunately, the highly respected Thai legal scholar Professor Dr Ukrit Mongkolnavin stepped forward to save the place. He had it dismantled and transported to Bangkok to serve as an education centre for the Devaraj Kunchorn Voraviharn Temple. The building's precious exterior with its ornate fretwork had to be preserved with UV-protective paint, so the natural golden glow of the timber is now masked with white paint.

The building opened to the public as a museum in 2009, and two of the upper-storey rooms house life-size and unnervingly life-like sculptures of 36 celebrated patriarch monks, sitting cross-legged in their saffron robes. One of the monks is Luang Phor Thuad, who is said to have been so holy that he turned seawater to freshwater when he walked on it.

Shards of red stone that are said to have been Buddha's blood

There are also small bowls holding what are said to be relics of Buddha in the form of dozens of little splinters of bones, and under one of the shrines, shards of red stone that are said to have been Buddha's blood.

Another teak treasure

The Giant Swing is Bangkok's other great teak monument. The swing's two main supports are single teak logs over 21.15 metres long and more than 3.5 metres each in circumference. For more on this see p. 32.

WAT RATCHATHIWAT

A peaceful temple for quiet contemplation

3 Samsen Road, Dusit
Daily 8am–6pm

I t is easy to get temple-fatigue in Bangkok, where the jostling hordes of tourists and clammy tropical air can turn a temple visit into a less-than-spiritual experience. Of course, not all are as busy as Wat Pho (one of the oldest and largest Buddhist temples in the city), and the wonderfully quiet Wat Ratchathiwat is a fantastic option for those who want to witness the true tranquillity of a Buddhist temple. Wat Ratchathiwat is on the banks of the Chao Phraya River – it is surrounded by old trees and manicured gardens, and the vast stillness here creates a real sanctuary within the busyness of Bangkok.

In the mornings after they have completed *bin ta baht* (see p. 82), the monks gather in the *ubosot* (ordination hall) at Wat Ratchathiwat and you can hear their chanting wafting through the gardens. Visitors are welcome inside when the monks have left the *ubosot* (usually around 8.30am) – it is an evocative place to sit in stillness. Surrounding the entire ubosot is a fresco designed by Prince Naris and created by the Italian artist Carlo Regoli – the paintings depict the *Wessandon Chadok*, a collection of stories from Theravada Buddhism.

The large temple complex was once the residence of Rama IV, who lived at this temple for seven of the 27 years of his monastic life, when he was Prince Mongkut (see p. 72 and p. 237). It was initially built during the Ayutthaya Period, when it was known as Wat Samorai, but has undergone many renovations over the years and today contains an interesting assortment of buildings – the large Dhamma Hall, built during the reign of Rama V (1868 to 1910), is regarded as the most beautiful golden teak building in Thailand. In the grounds is an intriguing garden area that is dotted with images of Buddhas, gods and sages. Give yourself at least an hour to wander these temple grounds and soak up the atmosphere.

The prince who was a master-craftsman

Prince Narisara Nuwattiwong (1863–1947) – or Prince Naris – was a son of Rama IV. He was a scholar and prolific artist often celebrated as "the Great Craftsman of Siam". Some important works include Wat Benchamabophit (the Marble Temple), which he designed; the royal anthem *Sansoen Phra Barami*, for which he wrote the lyrics; and the crests of various government ministries, which he designed. He also designed the Pig Memorial (see p. 52).

CONCEPTION CHURCH

⑦

The oldest Catholic church in Bangkok

167 Soi Mitrakam (near Soi Samsen 11 and Soi Samsen 13), off Samsen Road, Dusit
Daily 5am–8.30pm

The regal façade of the Conception Church faces the Chao Phraya River, as do all buildings erected in the days when waterways were the region's main transport route. From the façade, a statue of the Virgin Mary looks out over the approaching congregation, and on Sunday mornings recorded bells chime from the bell tower, ringing out across the neighbourhood. The high wooden ceilings of the nave, supported by six teak pillars, allow Thai hymns to soar before filtering out into the humid Bangkok air.

The Romanesque church looks narrow and linear from the river, but it stretches back into the elegantly curved sacristy that was the entire church when it was founded in 1674, almost a century before Bangkok was established. The church was built when French bishop Louis Laneau, head of the Roman Catholic mission in Indochina, was based in Ayutthaya. At that time about 2,000 Christians lived in the Siamese capital, and Portuguese missionaries established a smaller settlement 70 km downriver, where the Conception Church stands today. They believed it was a strategic location from which they could reach out into the small surrounding communities and convert Siamese people to their religion. (See p. 188 for more on the Portuguese settlers.)

For a while the area around the church was called Baan Portugal (the "Portuguese Village"), but in 1785, after a small group of Christians fled persecution in Cambodia and settled here, people started to refer to the area as Baan Khmer, a name it still carries today.

Six decades after the arrival of the Cambodians, Vietnamese refugees arrived in the area and the community outgrew the small chapel. Under the supervision of Jean-Baptiste Pallegoix (see p. 235), the French bishop who was head of the congregation at that time, the church was extended in 1874 to create the building you see today.

The sturdy, white-walled Conception Church – also called the Church of Immaculate Conception and Wat Khamen – is the oldest Catholic church in Bangkok. In this predominantly Buddhist country less than half a percent of the population is Catholic, and the church stands in a neighbourhood where signs of Catholicism reign: photographs of the Pope are framed and displayed outside some homes, while others host small, colourful shrines to the Virgin Mary.

ST FRANCIS XAVIER CHURCH (8)

A church built for Vietnamese refugees

Soi Samsen 11, off Samsen Road, Dusit
Mass: Weekdays 6am and 7pm; Sundays 6.30am, 8.30am, 10am and 4pm

The approach to St Francis Xavier Church from Samsen Road will leave you with little doubt that you are walking towards a place of worship, but it is the grand square at the front of the church, next to the river, that gives this stately building its presence. This building is, however, more than simply a church – it is a tribute to religious tolerance and cross-cultural friendship in Thailand.

In the early 1830s, 1,350 Vietnamese Catholics asked Rama III for his protection when they fled religious persecution in their own country. The king not only granted them some land, but he also donated money to build a bamboo church. That church was destroyed by a storm three years later, and then replaced by a wooden one.

At that time French bishop Jean-Baptiste Pallegoix was based nearby at the Conception Church (see p. 234), and he was a close friend of the king's younger brother, Prince Mongkut. When the prince ascended to the throne as Rama IV (see p. 72), he was aware that the Catholic community in the Samsen area had grown considerably, and so donated more land for a larger church.

The new church – inaugurated in 1867 – was named in honour of Saint Francis Xavier, the Spanish missionary who travelled extensively in Asia in the first half of the 1500s.

A statue from Florence

On the Samsen Road side of the church there is a bronze statue of Jesus giving sight to a blind man. Rama V, the first Thai monarch to travel to Europe, bought the statue from a foundry in Florence during a trip to Europe in 1897.

The extraordinary friendship between a Catholic bishop and a Buddhist monk

During the 27-year reign of Rama III, the king's younger brother, Prince Mongkut (1804–1868), was a monk who for some time lived at Wat Ratchathiwat (see p. 230), close to the Conception Church (see p. 234) where French bishop Jean-Baptiste Pallegoix (1805–1862) was based. The monk and the bishop struck up a close friendship, and as well as discussing science and mathematics, the two men taught each other the language of their scriptures – Latin and Pali. Pallegoix authored the first Siamese-French-English dictionary, which can be seen online at archive.org.

MUSEUM OF FLORAL CULTURE

A beautiful, tranquil space that makes for a captivating visit

315 Samsen Road Soi 28, Yeak Soi Ongkarak 13, Dusit
floralmuseum.com
Tuesday to Sunday, 10am–6pm

The Museum of Floral Culture is a charming oasis dedicated to the art, history and roles that flowers play within South-East Asian cultures. The museum's exhibits are inside an old colonial-style tropical home, a teak building almost hidden from view by an abundance of trees, palms and orchids. It is a beautiful, tranquil space that makes for a captivating visit.

Flowers are an integral part of Thai culture: they are used in religious and cultural ceremonies, as well as for decorations, gifts and religious offerings, and almost always, the flowers carry meaning and are connected to myths or symbolism. The Museum of Floral Culture showcases these flowers along with elaborate flower-arranging examples, techniques and traditions from Thailand, India, Laos, Myanmar, Japan and Bali.

In Thailand the delicate art of floral arrangements often involves painstakingly folding and threading petals and buds to create different forms, and you can try to create some of these at the museum. A garland of jasmine buds, called a *malai*, is one of the most common arrangements: it is used as an offering in temples and also as a welcome gift for guests. Another form of floral art commonly seen around Bangkok is the *khruang khwaen*, a floral pendant that is used to scent a room. It can be created in many different shapes and sizes, and the museum has beautiful examples that look like chandeliers and lace netting.

The small shop and a quiet tearoom at the museum offer a chance to relax after a tour of the museum, which is accessible only with a guide.

Why is yellow considered a royal colour?

Thailand's national tree and flower, *ratchaphruek* or golden shower tree (*Cassia fistula*), erupts into bloom around the end of March, when golden yellow flowers hang from the branches like delicate bunches of grapes. It was chosen as a national symbol during the reign of Rama IX (1946 to 2016), who was born on a Monday.

In Thailand each day of the week is associated with a colour, and Monday is yellow, which is why yellow is considered a royal colour. A spectacular place to see the trees in flower is Queen Sirikit Park (see p. 245), which also has an abundance of flame and tabebuia trees (*Delonix regia* and *Tabebuia rosea*), usually in bloom in March and April.

CHATUCHAK PLANT MARKET

Horticultural feng shui: a mini guide to buying lucky plants

Kamphaeng Phet 2 Road, Chatuchak
Wednesday and Thursday 7am–6pm

While Chatuchak Weekend market is world famous, few people are aware of the unusual market that takes place on its south-western fringe each Wednesday and Thursday. Much more than a mere plant market, this is where the people of Bangkok come to stock up on botanic karma.

The main market – boasting 15,000 stalls and attracting about 200,000 people each weekend – is famous as the largest market on the planet. The plant market, meanwhile, has about half a kilometre of stalls selling everything from lacy air-plants to full-sized frangipani trees ... and it might be the best place on the planet to buy lucky plants.

Feng shui plays a huge part in many aspects of Thai life, and at Chatuchak on Wednesdays and Thursdays you will see people selecting plants according to their feng shui properties. Just as the right choice of plant is believed to promote growth, development and prosperity in the home or workplace, the wrong type (or careless positioning) can provoke weakness and ill-health.

Bamboo is one of the most powerful plants: it embodies long life and tenacity, and its powers are said to be so pervasive that merely hanging a painting of bamboo will exorcise evil from a house. Plum trees too represent tenacity, since even withered branches frequently continue to blossom. With its tough, spreading branches, jasmine is believed to strengthen family bonds, and mother-in-law's tongue – resembling the spear of the god Indra – is a protection against evil. *Kum* (Chinese for orange) sounds very similar to *kim*, the Chinese word for gold, so for this reason alone the plant is propitious, and the fruit is a popular offering in Chinese temples.

Feng shui is far from a dying belief and in fact seems to be continuously evolving with the times: bromeliads have become popular since a belief was spawned that they absorb radiation from computer screens. Positioning is important and experts say that the plants are best kept on the left-hand side of your desk. Cacti are also believed to act as a radiation screen, but they are often avoided because thorns bring negative energy into the home. Thorny plants like bougainvillea or roses outside the home function as a protective shield, but they can also act as obstacles and challenges in your public life.

SIAMESE FIGHTING FISH AT CHATUCHAK MARKET

Feisty flashes of fishy fieriness

Kamphaeng Phet 4 Road, Chatuchak
Daily, 8am–6pm

The Chatuchak Weekend Market covers an area the size of 20 soccer pitches. It is the world's largest market, but the quieter northern edge, a stretch that is open throughout the week, claims another record: in 2019 a Siamese fighting fish with colour markings resembling the Thai flag was sold here for 53,500 baht (about US$1,750).

The stalls here form the aquarium section of the market, and it is obvious from the vivid splashes of colour why the highly territorial betta fish (as Siamese fighting fish are properly known – or *Betta splendens*) are often called "jewels of the Orient". In the wild these fish are relatively dull in colour and only exhibit their vibrant hues when they are agitated, but breeders have managed to make the colours permanent. The idea that fish have only a three-second memory is a myth, and recent studies have shown that these little Siamese warriors suffer stress due to being kept for long periods next to neighbours they regard as territorial threats. Some fish here are in plastic bags while others are in tiny aquariums, and would-be purchasers test their potential purchases for aggressiveness simply by dipping the bagged specimens into one of these "solitary confinement cells".

Many of the fish in this market sell for less than a dollar and are viewed as easy starter pets, but experts say they require more complex caring than most people imagine. Under ideal conditions a betta fish could live for up to 10 years, but sadly few last more than a couple of months.

A fishy form of feng shui

Other specimens here are sold exclusively to devotees of a fishy form of feng shui. Feng shui fish are particularly prized by many Thai Chinese and there is a complex symbolism regarding colours and appearance. For example, look out for the relatively privileged fat little goldfish that are shaped like golden coins – they will be nurtured and protected, and will hopefully lead a long life since they are said to represent the wealth of their owner. The long, daggerlike black fish, however, are likely to live less blessed lives since they represent any misfortune that might enter the household ... and it is therefore to be hoped that they die swiftly, taking the bad luck with them.

On Bang Ka Chao Peninsula, just south of Bangkok, you wi' world's only Siamese Fighting Fish Gallery (open only ? 10am–5pm; fightingfishgallery.com).

BANGKOK BUTTERFLY GARDEN

Airborne jewels near the world's largest market

Bangkok Butterfly Garden and Insectarium
Kamphaengpet 3 Road, Lad Yao, Chatuchak
Tuesday to Sunday 8.30am–4.30pm

As you wander beside the waterfalls and toiletries in the Bangkok Butterfly Garden, you will see an enthralling selection of Thailand's beautiful orchids along with butterflies of every colour and size imaginable.

The country's wealth in orchids (totalling about 1,000 species) is surpassed by its butterfly numbers: of the world's estimated 20,000 butterfly species, about 1,100 occur in Thailand. Wandering around this butterfly garden, it is easy to believe, and although there are only about 20 species of butterflies in this 1,300-square-metre dome, there are hundreds upon hundreds of the beautiful creatures flitting about.

Look out for the Paris Peacock, the elegant Malay Lacewing or the enchanting Spotted Jay (with translucent "windows" set into its wings). Tiny Lime Blues and Siam Tree Nymphs shimmer like gems and Giant Silkworm Butterflies and Golden Birdwings flutter their 15-cm wingspans. You will also see chrysalises, and if you stay long enough, you might actually see a butterfly emerging. More than just a butterfly garden, this is an entire habitat, and you will see frogs and tadpoles in the ponds and colourful lizards and geckos among the rocks.

Other peaceful parks to visit

If this natural profusion provides inspiration, you will not have to look far for some wonderfully peaceful parks – idyllic antidotes to the clamour of Bangkok. The rolling meadows of Wachirabenchathat Park (where the Bangkok Butterfly Garden and Insectarium is located) were once the fairways of the State Railway golf course, and just across the road you will find Chatuchak Park with its serpentine lake. The lovely Queen Sirikit Park (just to the south) has particularly pretty avenues, constructed islands and botanical gardens with shrubs and trees all labelled in both Thai and English. It is a spectacular place to be when the trees are in bloom (see p. 238). You are sure to see a whole plethora of butterflies in these parks that together form a green space with more than 6 km of pretty walkways and cycling paths. (Cycles are available for hire from about 20 baht for three hours). These parks – and the Butterfly Garden – are just a 10-minute walk from Chatuchak Weekend Market and make for a picturesque post-shopping picnic stop.

CHAOMAE THAPTHIM SHRINE

One of Bangkok's most enthralling buildings

Soi Phibunsongkhram 15, Suan Yai, Nonthaburi
Daily 8am–6pm

With golden dragons clambering up every pillar, and mythical creatures entwined across its sweeping roof, Chaomae Thapthim Shrine might be the most colourful Chinese temple in Bangkok. Despite its position right next to the Nonthaburi Museum (see p. 248), very

few visitors ever explore this riverside shrine, which is dedicated to the Chinese goddess of the sea. It is well patronised, however, by residents of this little-known quarter – specifically of Chinese descent – and no matter what time you visit it is likely to be swirling with shifting clouds of incense. Access is prohibited to those not praying, but you will be invited to watch from the courtyard, which offers a good view of the main shrine.

During the reign of Rama V (1868 to 1910), many Chinese settled in this outlying part of the city in response to a royal drive to enhance rice farming north of Bangkok, on the banks of the Chao Phraya River. In 1888 a new steamship line started between Hainan island (near Hong Kong) and Bangkok, cutting the voyage time to about a week and increasing the influx massively until, by the 1920s, an average of almost 300 Chinese a day were arriving in the city. Many of these immigrants came to dig irrigation channels and transportation canals, but those who managed to save some capital often chose Nonthaburi as home and became rice-farmers or traders. There were very few Chinese women, so in many cases the immigrants married local women and founded families that are fully integrated into Thai life, but who still practise their own style of Buddhism at Chaomae Thapthim Shrine.

In *Siamese Melting Pot: Ethnic Minorities in the Making of Bangkok* (Silkworm Books, 2017), Edward Van Roy wrote that "the Hainanese built at each of their settlements a single large shrine devoted to Tian Fa, Empress of Heaven and protector of seamen". While the Teochew Chinese community – with their residential settlements farther downriver

(see p. 206) – were considered formidable businessmen and grew powerful thanks to their brotherhoods and secret societies, the Hainanese were adventurers and explorers. From Nonthaburi they headed farther upcountry and established trade networks for timber, rice, hides and other jungle produce. Nonthaburi's shrine was enriched through the generations with each successful voyage or trading venture. The end result, as we see today, is one of Bangkok's most enthralling buildings.

MUSEUM OF NONTHABURI

One of Bangkok's most charming timber buildings

Tambon Suan Yai, Nonthaburi
Tuesday to Friday 9am–5pm; Saturday and Sunday 10am–6pm

The Museum of Nonthaburi provides a deep understanding of an area that was nicknamed "City of Happiness". With a history that dates to 1549, the northern suburb of Nonthaburi is a fascinating one, and this museum sheds light on the diverse communities that settled here, the traditional pottery created here, the lush orchards Nonthaburi was known for, and the intriguing history of this stately heritage building.

The informative museum, which has beautiful fretwork along its 150-metre façade, also offers a wonderful chance to explore the interior of one of Bangkok's most charming timber buildings. Built in 1910, it served as Kings College boarding school until it closed due to financial difficulties in 1925, then as Nonthaburi City Hall until 1992, and finally as a training institute for the Ministry of the Interior. The ornately carved verandas are now cracked and worn, like the foundation make-up of a venerable old dame. If anything, this adds to the atmospheric grandeur, and you still catch a sense of what – in other parts of Asia – is usually known as the "colonial era".

Through the shrewd diplomacy of its rulers, old Siam avoided the pillaging of European imperial rule that blotted the history books of every other country in the region, but this does not mean that the city (and Nonthaburi in particular) was not heavily influenced by foreign cultures. The museum outlines the often painful background of a whole host of diverse Nonthaburi communities, including Mon from Myanmar, Muslims from the Malay Peninsula and the Hokkien, Cantonese and Hakka immigrants from China, who were hired to dig canals and work in the famous orchards.

A tribute to the old orchards

Nonthaburi was always known for producing succulent plum mangos, and the most delicious durians in the country. On the riverside walkway in front of the Museum of Nonthaburi you might be astonished to see what appear to be durians hanging, like spiked cannonballs, from every lamppost. These very lifelike decorations testify to the nationwide fame of Nonthaburi's celebrated *kan yao* (long-stem durians).

BANG KRASO STILTED VILLAGE ⑮

A delightful place to wander and soak up an
atmosphere of days gone by

Off Nonthaburi Soi 11, Bang Kraso, Nonthaburi

The Chao Phraya might be lauded as the River of Kings, but not everybody who lives along its banks is quite so privileged. The Muslim village at Bang Kraso, a labyrinth of around 500 stilted houses built along a web of boardwalks, offers a glimpse into the realities of what used to be everyday life along the river.

Bangkok evolved around waterways, and living on or above the river and canals used to be the norm (see p. 22) – it was only during the reign of Rama IV (1851 to 1868) that the first "real" road was constructed. As the city evolved, many of the smaller canals were covered over or filled in and replaced by roads, but take a boat along the river and through some of the *khlongs* (canals) and you will see remnants of the city's amphibious past.

Bang Kraso's silver-domed mosque is built on solid land next to the cemetery (with all the headstones, as always, oriented towards

Mecca) – however, the mosque provides the main point of entry to one of Bangkok's last stilted-village communities. Bang Kraso is a delightful place to wander and soak up an atmosphere of days gone by. Stop at one of the neighbourhood vendors and grab a cup of strong coffee and some delicious *kanom krok* (coconut-custard puddings), and you are likely to see passing women carrying packets of market-bought produce, laundry hanging over windowsills, plants growing outside doorways in old paint pots, and old men fishing from stilted platforms – simple, everyday life unfolding. Some of the most evocative timber houses here feature fine fretwork, Islamic-style arches and shady verandas that allow the inhabitants to chat to passers-by and have conversations with neighbours across the narrow alleys.

It is often estimated that around 5 percent of Bangkok's population is Muslim. In his informative 2017 study *Siamese Melting Pot: Ethnic Minorities in the Making of Bangkok* (Silkworm Books, 2017), Edward Van Roy explains that "the Muslim minority has traditionally been referred to collectively – sometimes pejoratively – as *khaek isalam*, literally 'Muslim guests' or 'strangers'". Spend a while exploring the colourful community of Bang Kraso, and you are likely to feel that you are among friends rather than strangers.

KO KRET POTTERY

The village where Mother Earth is transformed into fine art

Tambon Ko Kret, Nonthaburi
Daily 8am–4pm

It was in the 18th century that Mon refugees chose little Ko Kret island in the Chao Phraya River as their home because of the excellent quality of its clay: they founded one of Thailand's greatest surviving craft traditions there.

The Mon arrived from what is now Myanmar as early as 1774. Initially they produced relatively simple earthenware pots that they used to barter for produce from neighbouring farmers, but their reputation as potters grew until the finest pieces were being distributed throughout the country. The people of Ko Kret were renowned for a variety of pots that they produced: the unusually thin earthenware rice pots that enhanced heat distribution and allowed the fragrance of smoke to reach the rice; the large *kradi* curry-pots (from which to feed crowds during ceremonies); and small *katha* pots (like Thai-style fondues). They also made special pots for holding medicinal concoctions, decorated with twisted bamboo motifs to ward off black magic. Even today, during festivals, you might see musicians on Ko Kret playing the traditional earthenware drums known as *thon*.

The finest pieces of Ko Kret craftsmanship are the lidded water containers once reserved for Mon royal families, which have since become an icon of the island. With exquisitely sculpted lids and ornate stands (initially designed to prevent moisture gathering when placed on a wooden floor), these days they are usually made only as temple offerings or as tributes to important people. (A fine example can be seen at Museum of Nonthaburi – see p. 248.)

During the industry's heyday in the late 1950s, there were as many as 100 family-run factories on the island, but the production was a lengthy process with initial clay-trampling by water buffalo taking up to five days, and the actual firing lasting more than 20 days. Of more than 40 large brick kilns that were once operating here, only about half a dozen are still in use. You can still walk into the empty kilns and see the offerings which give thanks to the ancestors and ask forgiveness from Mother Earth for plundering her clay deposits.

MADAME BREAST-SLAPPER

A hands-on "beauty treatment" to get rid of wrinkles or increase breast size

90 Soi Ram Intra 65, Tha Raeng, Bang Khen
By appointment only: 086 535 5999 or 0945 655 888
30,000 baht for a face-slapping treatment; 18,000 baht for breast-slapping

One of the quirkiest beauty treatments in Bangkok must be "slapping", a procedure mastered by Khemmikka Na Songkhla (better known as Khunying Tobnom – Madame Breast-slapper), a former model who learned the technique from her grandmother. "Slapping" is just as it sounds – the beautician hits the body with her hands to tone facial muscles and get rid of wrinkles, change face shape, or increase breast size.

A visit to Khunying Tobnom's treatment rooms is like stepping into another (rather bizarre) world. The reception area is bursting with Jujok idols (she hopes to get into the *Guinness Book of Records* for the world's largest collection) – there are photographs of clients, images of Ganesha, and the air is filled with the shrill sounds of Thai pop music. But it is Khunying Tobnom herself that makes the place feel quite other-worldly – there is just something about her that makes wearing a plastic parrot on her head seem quite natural. "I started off by slapping breasts to make them bigger and firmer," explains Khunying Tobnom, who has been slapping for more than 30 years, and claims to have increased her own breast size by four inches: "I learnt it from my grandmother, who adapted it from traditional Thai medicine."

The authors of this book had a session with Khunying Tobnom, who delivered slaps with the back of her hands to the rhythm of a song (she had once sung in a music video, which was playing on repeat while she worked). There were slight changes to the shape of our faces and breasts, but these did not last more than an hour.

According to *The Independent* newspaper, the technique, where fat is shifted around the body through strategically placed slaps, comes with a government stamp of approval.

In 2003 one of Khunying Tobnom's clients blamed breast-slapping for the onset of her breast cancer, and so the Institute of Thai and Alternative Medicine conducted a study into the technique. Over three months, 40 women between the ages of 20 and 60 underwent regular vigorous breast massages, and after three months, their breasts were "measurably larger", according to *The Independent*, and none of them developed breast cancer during that time. The study, which is not available to the public, is held in a private library at the Department of Thai Traditional and Alternative Medicine, and in Khunying Tobnom's home.

ROYAL THAI AIR FORCE MUSEUM

A spectacular collection of almost 100 rare flying machines

171 Phahonyothin Road, Don Mueang
museum.rtaf.mi.th
Note: If arriving by taxi, approach from the south on Phahonyothin Road – the northern access is forbidden for taxis beyond an air force guard-point
Tuesday to Sunday 8am–3.30pm; closed on holidays

The spectacular Royal Thai Air Force Museum is packed with intriguing flying machines and enough fascinating insights into Thai aviation history to keep you enthralled for several hours. Many exhibits here are

surprisingly accessible, and there can be few aircraft museums where you have an opportunity to get so close to such heavyweight artefacts.

Treasures of the collection include a rare Curtiss Hawk III biplane and the last surviving Vought O2U Corsair biplane. Built in 1934, the Corsair apparently had what must then have been a mindboggling maximum speed of 190 mph, but such figures pale into insignificance alongside the nearby 1961 F-86F Sabre fighter (with a maximum speed of 670 mph) and a 1998 Northrop Freedom Fighter capable of over 1,000 mph.

Most information boards throughout the museum are in Thai and English and, while there is plenty of technical data to delight even the most tech-savvy aviation buff, there are enough quirky background details to intrigue casual visitors. Of particular interest are the displays and aircraft relating to the birth of Thai aviation: Bangkok's first landing strip was at the spot where Siam Square now stands, and the very first Thai airplane (built in 1913) was apparently not a success – according to a museum signboard, "it could only move on ground".

Innovative Thai engineers learned to combine homegrown materials (sea hemp, willow, Indian mahogany, ivory and bamboo resin) with imported engines, and after what must have been a rocket-propelled learning-curve, a fearless pilot by the name of Lieutenant Colonel Phra Chalermkas made the first test flight in a Thai airplane on 24 May 1915.

Visitors to the museum are able to climb through and explore the instrument-studded cockpits of numerous planes and helicopters. Stand in the padded belly of an Alenia transporter, and it is easy to summon up a vaguely uneasy feeling – a hint of the butterflies that must have plagued paratroopers who were flying into battle. Other substantially less sturdy flying machines, meanwhile, utterly defy imagination. Look out for one that seems to be little more than a plastic seat mounted underneath an oversized wall-fan, with the fuel-tank for an armrest.

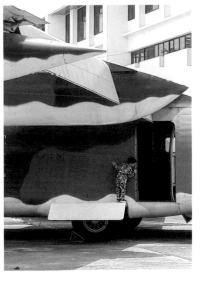

WAT PHRA DHAMMAKAYA

One of the most astounding religious complexes on our planet

23 Khlong Sam, Pathum Thani
en.dhammakaya.net

The *Guinness Book of Records* ranks Java's Borobudur temple complex as the largest Buddhist temple in the world, but Wat Phra Dhammakaya, with congregations rising to 200,000 people, is often said to be the largest temple of any kind in the world.

Your first sight of Wat Phra Dhammakaya might be from the landing approach to Don Mueang Airport, and from the air you might imagine that a gigantic golden UFO has landed in an immense parking lot. When you get closer, walking across the sun-baked expanse of the Maharatanaviharnkot Meditation Square (half a kilometre wide), you will see that the gold surface of the Dhammakaya Cetiya dome is covered with small stylised statues of Buddhas. In their minimalistic modernity they also look like an army of aliens, and there are said to be a million of them covering the surface of the dome (although those who have taken time to count, claim that it is more like 300,000). These 15-cm-tall statues are made of silicon bronze and gold particles, and each image is engraved with the name of a donor. The *New York Times* estimated the cost of these alone to be about US$90-million. The whole dome is then topped with a pure silver Grand Buddha image weighing 14 tonnes.

While during important Buddhist festivals such as Makha Bucha as many as 100,000 people will be at this temple, on a "regular" day you are quite likely to have one of the most astounding religious complexes on our planet all to yourself.

You might be tempted to drop a few notes into one of the many donation boxes that are temptingly marked "Path to Heaven".

So, just how big is this place?
The immense Dhammakaya Assembly Hall, the first building you will enter, is so incredibly large that the floor is polished by cleaners dragging brooms on the back of motorbikes.

The "longest journey walking on flower petals"
In 2015 pilgrim monks officially broke the *Guinness Book of Records* world record for the "longest journey walking on flower petals". 1,130 monks walked for 29 days across 485 km of petals that had been strewn by well-wishers along the Thai highways leading to Wat Phra Dhammakaya.

....
....
....
....
....
....
....
....
....
....
....
....
....
....
....
....
....
....
....
....
....
....
....
....
....
....
....

NOTES

NOTES

NOTES

NOTES

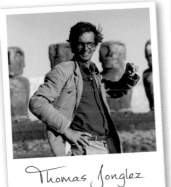

Thomas Jonglez

It was September 1995 and Thomas Jonglez was in Peshawar, the northern Pakistani city 20 kilometres from the tribal zone he was to visit a few days later. It occurred to him that he should record the hidden aspects of his native city, Paris, which he knew so well. During his seven-month trip back home from Beijing, the countries he crossed took in Tibet (entering clandestinely, hidden under blankets in an overnight bus), Iran and Kurdistan. He never took a plane but travelled by boat, train or bus, hitch-hiking, cycling, on horseback or on foot, reaching Paris just in time to celebrate Christmas with the family.

On his return, he spent two fantastic years wandering the streets of the capital to gather material for his first "secret guide", written with a friend. For the next seven years he worked in the steel industry until the passion for discovery overtook him. He launched Jonglez Publishing in 2003 and moved to Venice three years later. In 2013, in search of new adventures, the family left Venice and spent six months travelling to Brazil, via North Korea, Micronesia, the Solomon Islands, Easter Island, Peru and Bolivia. After seven years in Rio de Janeiro, he now lives in Berlin with his wife and three children.

Jonglez Publishing produces a range of titles in nine languages, released in 40 countries.